W9-AER-713

The Presenter's Fieldbook

The Presenter's Fieldbook

by Robert J. Garmston
with Illustrations by Michael Buckley

Christopher-Gordon Publishers, Inc.
Norwood, Massachusetts

Credits

Every effort has been made to contact copyright holders for permission to reproduce borrowed material where necessary. We apologize for any oversights and would be happy to rectify them in future printings.

Excerpts from "Paddling Together: A Copresenting Primer," copyright © 1988, *Training & Development,* American Society for Training and Development, reprinted with permission. All rights reserved.

Excerpts for "Staff Developers as Social Architects," copyright © 1991, Educational Leadership, reprinted with permission.

Material originally appearing in *The Developer* and *Journal for Staff Development* reprinted with permission of The National Staff Development Council.

Excerpt from "The Little Boy" used with permission of the author, Helen Buckley.

Christopher-Gordon Publishers, Inc.
480 Washington Street
Norwood, MA 02062
Tel: 617-762-5577

Printed in the United States of America

10 9 8 7 6 5 4 3 2 1 02 01 00 99 98 97

ISBN: 0-926842-65-X

To my wise and loving mother and father,
Alice Mather Hart and Charles King Hart.
I am fortunate and blessed to have you as parents.

VIEW

TABLE OF CONTENTS

FIGURES

ACKNOWLEDGMENTS

I am grateful to many people for allowing me to be a continuing student of their expertise in presenting to adults and for providing me with opportunities to practice, explore, and write about my learning. Among these are Art Costa and my exceptionally skillful colleagues at the Institute for Intelligent Behavior; friends in many districts and on boards who have invited me to work with them; and thousands of knowledgeable and committed professionals, paraprofessionals and parents with whom I have learned in workshop settings. I am particularly indebted to Bruce Wellman, my co-author in *How to Make Presentations that Teach and Transform* (1992); Suzanne Bailey, presentation and change-agent virtuoso, with whom I have had the privilege of copresenting many times; Frank Koontz of the Bureau of Education and Research, from whom I have learned much about presenting to large groups; Dennis Sparks and Paul Burden at the National Council for Staff Development, who have encouraged, edited, and supported these efforts over time.

I am also indebted to others who have been islands of strength, friendship, inspiration, and support closer to home. Of special note is Debbi Miller, who cheerfully and skillfully represents me to others, untiringly organizes and supports the work that emerges from my office, and is unquestionably my right, left, and best brain. A loving thanks to my capable and talented youngest daughter, Wendy, who helped with the final editing.

My deepest appreciation goes to my wife, Sue. Out of our relationship grows the wellspring of my energies and my deepest source of learning. Thank you.

PREFACE

Many of these thoughts appeared originally in National Staff Development Council publications: some of them in *The Developer*, others in the *Journal of Staff Development*. Another appeared originally in *Educational Leadership*, another in the *Training and Development Journal;* still others first saw print at California State University, Sacramento in support of professors engaged in a Professors' Peer Coaching Program. Some of the ideas are being published for the first time. While this is a collection of occasional pieces—edited, enriched, and extended in this publication—there is nothing haphazard about their relationship. They are linked firmly together by a chain of values and assumptions about adult learners and the school organizations in which educators work.

Since most of these writings found their first expression in a personal journal format, the word *I* appears many times. Viewed together in this collection, the frequency of the personal pronoun may seem overdone and self-centered. I hope readers will overlook this impression, should it surface for them, and interpret the personalization as originally intended: the candid report of the struggles of one person's continuing journey in learning effective presenting.

This book takes the view that a presentation's greatest importance lies not in the skills and knowledge that participants might gain from a particular session, but in the contribution those skills, knowledge, and attitudes make to the broader dynamics of the work culture. Teachers' thoughts, feelings, decisions, and behaviors are influenced more by the culture of the workplace than by teachers' skills, knowledge, and prior or current training. As the work culture of schools change, so will schools.

Schools *must* change. Members of a school cafeteria staff in a school I know met recently for in-service training. One was in her seventies, another was in her fifties, and a third was in her late twenties. They had all attended the same school as children and agreed that since their attendance, nothing significant in their school had changed.

Schools are indeed changing. In many communities throughout North America, faculties are rethinking the organization of the school, deepening their knowledge of academic disciplines, incorporating principles of constructivist learning into daily classroom instruction, and learning to work together to set standards, solve problems, and improve learning experiences for all students.

This collection of writings describes how to structure and deliver presentations that are intended to support such changes. Effective presentations honor participants as responsible, growing, autonomous, and interdependent adults. Presentations are a special type of intervention in an interactive and dynamic field of school change. The presentations described here presume good schools and the best audiences and artfully achieve the best for and with them. Such presentations help to put people in touch with their own genius. The presentation is an instrument of the presenter, who serves as a guide to adult learning and transformational change.

This book is written for any person in the educational setting who has an occasion to present to others. This includes the novice and the expert presenter, the teacher sharing expertise with colleagues, the staff developer refining his or her craft, and the administrator speaking to parents, fellow educators, or a board. For each, here are some tidbits, tips, and treasures to add to their presentation repertoire.

Robert Garmston
Spring 1997
El Dorado Hills, CA

CHAPTER 1 How to Present When You Wish to Transform

What is it that transforms? Sometime during the writing of this book, my wife Sue and I spent a month in East Africa. Most of that time was spent in Tanzania. We started in Dar Esalam on the Indian Ocean, where I worked with educators at the International School. From Dar we boated to Zanzibar, where we were delightfully lost in the sensations, sights, and sounds of a Muslim world of architecture, language, prayer calls, food, and history. Then we flew back to the mainland and this century, where we began an incredible eleven-day photographic safari in the Serengeti. We were guests in a Masai village, visited the archaeological site at Olduvai Gorge, which marks the very beginning of human life over 3.5 million years ago, and climbed to 15,500 feet on Mt. Kilimanjaro with a guide and four porters. Now I tell my friends that the experience was transforming. What do I mean?

I cannot ever again view the world in the same way or take life for granted. I see and hear birds now, in my own neighborhood or on the streets I walk in other cities. Here in my own country I am conscious of birds that are cousins of the flamboyant flamingo, the cory buzzard, the secretary bird, and the lilac-breasted roller, all of which still strut, fly, and preen in my mind's eye. I am filled with awe that lions and gazelles, leopards and wildebeests, predators and prey, should live in such easy distance of one another and that predators, unlike the human animal, are to be feared only when they are hungry. That the modern rural Tanzanian knows a way of life so different from ours causes me to question mine. The Masai, great keepers of cattle with homes made of brambles and cow dung, whose patterns of living are as unchanged as the migratory movements of the wildebeests following the short-grass plains during the rains, has me wondering who we are in the scope of things. I come from a "taker culture," which ravages the earth's resources for expansion and progress; they live on the land with the rhythms of the seasons, leaving the land as they find it.

We humans live in a world of our own making, constructed by our collective and individual mental models. Perhaps the greatest gift we can give one another is the opportunity to look beyond our current models, for any model has, along with its values, certain constraints and limitations. Our best work with one another is to transform, to transcend current perceptions and realities.

Presentations can have deep and lasting transformational significance. They can point us in the direction of worthwhile change and create, shape, and contribute to personal and group development long after the presentation itself is over. The ideas in this chapter address this bigger picture, the transforming nature of significant presentations and their defining attributes.

Staff Developers as Guides

Notes from a Safari Journal

We met our guide Juma at the Mt. Kilimanjaro International Airport near Arusha. When I commented on the intended length of our trip with him, he said, "We'll get to know each other very well."

A teacher recently wrote, "Up until two and a half years ago, I worked in an isolated school; however, I wasn't conscious of this fact. Things seemed to go quite well for me. The students enjoyed the lessons I prepared, I felt I was looked upon highly by both staff and administration, parents were delighted with what their students were learning, I had little difficulty developing lessons and securing materials, and I effectively dealt with problems that arose in my class. Granted, the principal was of little help and ruled with an iron fist, and lunchroom conversations focused on union activity and problem children, but this didn't concern me. I had few problems, and even though there were teachers whom I labeled ineffective, I was secure within my personal domain.

"It was only after I came to my present school that I realized how harmful and deadening this experience had been. I entered an environment where teacher-sharing was the norm, the principal empowered the teachers to make numerous school-wide decisions, and a technical culture flourished. There was in-service training on classroom problem-solving techniques and the best ways to assure student success. I found that many of my methods were outdated and ineffective, that complaining about students was reserved for just a few of the seventy-five faculty members, and that a sense of community was a necessity for those interested in being considered good teachers" (Pedersen, 1990).

The insights this teacher reports from his experience in two very different schools illustrate the need to be clear about our goals, roles, and basic assumptions about schools and staff development.

Staff development and presentations as we have known them are drawing their last breath. From the time of the first Teachers' Institute in Connecticut in 1839 to such recent and usefully crafted models as theory-demonstration-practice-coaching, the central emphasis has been on the teacher as a vessel to be filled; a figure to be instructed, enlightened, and molded into someone's image of a "good teacher." We can point to modest successes (Joyce and Showers, 1988), but even our recent refinements in staff development have not yet sufficiently altered the century old sameness of schooling or the destructive kind of pedagogical pluralism that exists in many schools. In these settings, many teachers work hard but in relative isolation, with different blueprints and stale tools. This contributes not only to school failure but to the continuing exodus of our most intellectually capable teachers. Nationally, half of our entering teachers have left the profession after five years.

However, not all schools are so stifled or stifling (Rosenholtz, 1989). Many brilliant exceptions exist in which deliberate, conscious leadership has served as a guide to schools as cultures of learning. Three terms need to be defined. A *guide* is one who points the way, scouting ahead yet traveling with the group through designated territory. *Culture* is a conscious pattern of values, actions, and artifacts. Being conscious, it is subject to our assessment and change. A *learning culture* is one in which "collaborative creativity in all contexts, relationships, and experiences is a basic purpose of the culture. It is a culture where the measure of success is the combined wisdom of groups and the synergy, leadership, and service of the organization as a whole" (Jaccaci, 1989). Schools and universities, according to Jaccaci, do not yet reflect this conception of a learning culture. "Although learning goes on in our schools and universities, it is primarily replicative learning aimed at passing along the intellectual and social agreements of the day to students."

I would amend Jaccaci's statement to read that *most* schools are not yet learning cultures. Fortunately, some schools are valuing that and learning how to do it.

The New Staff Development

The new staff development consists of support programs for new teachers, training in teaching methodologies, and the study of curricula. We will always need this, but to bring about the changes that probably all schools require, staff development must be much more. The new staff development requires guides, not gurus: guides with good maps of cultures of learning, rich knowledge, and instincts; guides that support teachers, administrators, classified staff, and resource personnel in learning together in self-reflective and creative ways, making the school experience a richer one for students.

Staff developers as guides know that adults develop best through engagement of their minds. They do this through solving problems and planning and developing programs and curricula with other professionals. Indeed, the richest staff development engages teachers as professionals and full partners in shaping the organization, governance, and curricula of schools. From this aspect of a learning culture, the school continually evolves as a more relevant and effective learning environment for students and the adults who work with them.

A word of caution is in order. Staff development that guides teacher engagement for the sake of engagement, or for the express goal of "restructuring," will not necessarily lead to better student learning. Most school reformers and practitioners take for granted that changes in structure produce changes in teaching practices, which in turn produce changes in student learning. However, research on these connections "presents a pessimistic and complex view" (Elmore, 1995).

Consider, for example, the manifestations of restructuring that one might think would lead to changes in teaching practices. A school could have many of the following changes in place with little effect on student learning (see Figure 1.1).

Changes in structure are only weakly related to changes in teaching practices. However—and this is the critical point—when the work of staff development is aimed at guiding the school's energies to focus the values and norms of attention on instruction, and when teachers take responsibility for student performance, the teacher empowerment that comes from restructuring efforts seems to lead to significant changes in teaching practices. These changes in teaching practices, in turn, seem to be related to improvements in student learning (Elmore, 1995).

The following structural changes may or may not lead to improvements in student learning:

- The school is governed by a site-based council composed of teachers, administrators, parents, and community members.
- Groups of teachers work together on a range of projects, including planning of common activities across groups and grades, development of curriculum units, and professional development to enhance their schools.
- Groups of teachers exercise control over discretionary resources that can be used to purchase new supplies and materials.
- On their own initiative, and with the cooperation of the principal and the endorsement of the site council, teachers have organized themselves into multiage teams, so students move flexibly among teachers within a team and are grouped according to their needs in a given subject.
- The planning time necessary for teachers to work in teams and to engage in curriculum development is created by coordinating teacher planning times, scheduling art and physical education so as to release teachers from regular classroom duties, and shortening one school day a week by an hour.

Figure 1.1: Structural Changes Only Weakly Related to Student Learning

Adapted from Richard Elmore, 1995

Therefore, while we previously have held the teaching of teachers (i.e., staff development) to be a unidirectional force affecting curriculum, instruction, and ultimately student learning, we are now witnessing a fresh reality. Collaboration, shared decision making, and the common and continual pursuit of changing norms, knowledge, and skills at the individual and organizational level are interrelated, multidirectional, and transformational forces that effect change in how and what students learn.

Today's staff developer is truly a guide whose territory is the culture of learning. The two dominant staff development tasks are the modification of the culture of the workplace and the modification of teachers' capacity to modify themselves. Teachers, along with principals and others, will develop as caretakers of caring communities and as collaborators, problem seekers, action researchers, and designers of responsive student-centered curricula in which students work harder, more meaningfully, and with more satisfaction than ever before. Michael Fullan (1993) says it well: All the good work being done in schools is merely tinkering unless we are changing the identity of all educators to be inquirers and collaborators. My friend Bruce Wellman would add that the focus of our inquiry must be grounded in the examination of student work and the teaching practices that improve it.

The new directions are not easy. While collaboration and shared decision making is essential to a learning culture, and perhaps to the survival of our system of schooling, it is also perilous. Of school faculties that have adopted participatory forms and have been exceptionally successful at increasing student learning, many have suffered frustration, exhaustion, and isolation.

Even so, there may be solace in knowing that beyond these troubled waters lies exceptional promise for American schools. There is no one formula, single approach, or universal strategy that exists to enter the world of schools as cultures of learning. The major questions are: What is the purpose and soul of this school? What do I have to contribute? How can we grow together for the improvement of student learning?

When the Presenter Is a Guide

I revel in this learning and relate Juma's role to my own when I am presenting. What is it about Juma that makes him such an

Notes from a Safari Journal

Somewhere in the Serengeti, Juma has led us to two female lions who are partially hidden in the tall grass, intently focused on a lone wildebeest just a few yards away. Juma consistently sees more than we do.

Yesterday, from the rim of Ngorongoro Crater, Juma pointed out elephants some 3,000 feet below, while we could barely make out dark shapes against the green fields. Later, we too can see elephants from a distance—not from quite as far away, but further than we'd ever imagined possible or useful. Now Juma adds distinctions and details: these are male, those are female; those trees have the bark rubbed off by them; and he tells us their more common name—Elly!

effective teacher and me such a successful learner in his presence? I believe it has more to do with what he knows about himself and what he values than what he knows about his topic.

To illustrate, I recently developed a workshop on "The Skillful Consultant." After presenting it the first time, I reflected on how it had gone. My mind was drawn to two things: an exercise that wildly exceeded my expectations and something that had not gone well. Of the two, the successful experience was more compelling to ponder. So with friend and colleague Marilyn Tabor as my coach, I examined the workshop to see what I could learn.

I was surprised that my insights were about me, not about teaching. By examining the "good" experience, I better understood my values, my intentions for participants' learning in the moment and in the future, and my own impassioned sense of mission toward these ends. Upon reflecting on the "bad" experience, I realized that my resolution of the problem focused on logistics, not values. I recognized that my ideals are often in conflict with "practical" goals, such as teaching skills or delivering information.

What about the Lions?

How does this relate to Juma and the lions? For Juma, finding the lions was not the important task; neither was naming them, allowing us to take pictures of them, or explaining how they hunted and what we were seeing. Juma, like all presenters, has many levels of goals as he works with learners. He might focus on:

- **Activities**
  We (participants and guide) will drive to the crater and look for lions.
  Participants will take a styles inventory and discuss the results.
- **Engagement**
  Bob and Sue will be excited.
  Participants will be energized and enjoy the session.
- **Content**
  Bob and Sue will learn the names of animals, or . . .
  Bob and Sue will understand the food chain, or . . .
  Bob and Sue will distinguish two types of gazelles.
  Participants will ask higher-order questions.

These three levels of presenter goals are always available to us as we plan and conduct presentations. Jon Saphier and Robert Gower (1987) believe that all classroom lessons should attain at least the third level, which they call *mastery.* The operating questions for a presenter working at level three would be: What will participants know or be able to do as a result of this presentation? How will I know they know it or can do it? Juma's goals, however, were beyond these and were transformational in nature. These are goals that Art Costa and I (Costa and Garmston, in press) envision as higher, more complex, and more empowering outcomes for instruction. Higher-order goals subsume the ones below them; that is, attainment of learning outcomes higher in the hierarchy automatically activate attainment of learning outcomes lower in the hierarchy.

The next two levels of presenter goals are:

- **Dispositions**
  Dispositions can include acquiring the ability to direct and control one's own learning, persistence, impulsivity, creativity, metacognition, communication, empathic listening, risk taking, and wonderment (Costa, 1991). For example, Bob and Sue will continue to learn after this trip, and participants will learn perseverance and collaboration.

- **Capacities**
  There are five human capacities, or mind states, that can be thought of as catalysts and energy sources fueling human accomplishment: efficacy, flexibility, craftsmanship, consciousness, and interdependence (Costa and Garmston, 1994). For example, Bob and Sue will see from richer perspectives, and participants will increase their capacity for self reflection.

The sixth presenter goal is more difficult to discuss. It is, however, an important quality that makes a presenter like a guide. Art and I call this level *ideals*.

- **Ideals**
  Learning at the level of ideals not only encompasses the mastery of thinking, dispositions, and capacities, but transcends these in pursuit of universal goals. These are the end states of the fully evolved human. In Jungian terms, this would be a stage of wisdom and integration. Robert Kegan (1992) might describe this as a stage of sufficient cognitive complexity in which the "illusion of our separateness" is shattered. For indigenous people throughout the world, it might be described as a oneness with the universe.

The presenter as guide must be faithful to external goals (i.e., goals for the program) as well as to universal goals (i.e., goodness, beauty, and unity).

As I think back on our eleven days together with Juma in the Serengeti, it seems that he was clear about what he valued in his work. If I were to think about it in educational terms, he wanted to provide learning experiences for all six levels of presenter goals discussed here. He helped us see the world in ways that were different from what would have been possible before the trip.

During our trip, I began to discern patterns in Juma's telling. He would often start big: "That's a gazelle." Later, he would say, "That's a Thomson's gazelle and that's a Grant's gazelle." Still later, watching another set of animals: "You can tell which is which by the black marking along the side of the Thomson." Even later: "There's a Tommy." Eventually, he would wait for us to name them. That is one way a presenter functions as a guide, revealing information about the territory at a pace appropriate for the adult learners on our safari.

At other times Juma explained the systems at work. "Of all the big cats, the lions exhibit the most cooperation during the hunt." Or: "The zebras travel with the wildebeests for protection."

Or: "There! See the Cape buffalo. Notice there are always egrets nearby. As this large and heavy animal moves, insects surface in the grass below. The birds depend on the buffalo for their food." Or: "See how the elephants, hippos, giraffes, gazelles and buffalo all share the same areas. They live together, yet each in its own way." Or: "Look. You are fortunate. There are some rhinos. They are nearly extinct because they are hunted for their horns."

On still other occasions, Juma helped me with my skills and my persistence. At the beginning of the trip, he would raise and lower the viewing roof or adjust the stepping plate to enter and exit the Land Rover. Later, he would encourage me to perform these tasks. Still later I would volunteer: "Juma, if you stop the car, I'll pull the top down." When what I did was incomplete, he would advise, "Lift up a little and pull down hard." He inspected to see that it was right.

As presenters, we are much like Juma in his role of guide. We know the territory, the roads, the distances, the travel times, the truck transporting us, the habitats and habits of the inhabitants, the predators and the prey, the grasses and the trees, the insects and the birds. But our knowledge of the territory—the content—comes alive and is useful in learning only to the degree that the audience's culture, interests, needs, and energy levels are known and we are capable of using this information for higher ends, toward dispositions, capacities and ideals. Juma was exquisitely tuned in to us. When we would tire, he would know. When we wanted to know, he would tell—but only then and only in an amount equal to our absorption capacity in the moment.

Please Mentor; Don't "Train the Trainer"

I now know why I've always been disturbed by "train the trainer" programs. They are designed to give teaching notes, time schedules, and overheads after a person has learned some new content. They are intended to support the person in training others in what they have learned, but the novice trainer cannot yet see what you see.

From Juma I learned that a guide will always see more than you. A guide's job is to help you see. When you can see as well as the guide, he or she is no longer a guide but a companion. A companion is one who keeps you company in traveling. This is a mutual benefit. This former guide, now companion, may see *differently* than you; that is the nature of different eyes and histories.

I'm sure we develop our best guides through programs of apprenticeship in mentoring. A "mentee" travels the road with you many times, talks with you, and acts with you, until he or she begins to see as much as you do. In this way, the "mentee," like an apprentice, learns all the secrets of the master and then adds his or her own. In contrast, train-the-trainer programs provide only a map of the territory, a listing of the animals within, their habits, some facts, and some cute things to say about each of them. The result is usually a poor-quality reproduction of the original.

Presentations That Transform

What distinguishes a transformational presentation—one that transforms the perspective or capacities of an audience—from an informational one? Why do some speaking events seem to produce energized, optimistic, on-fire audiences while others produce politeness? I've been talking with a number of colleagues[1] about these questions and am starting to believe that presenters operate much like Juma did, intuitively or consciously utilizing certain "macromaps" that make the difference.

A macromap looks at the long view, the large picture, in order to understand the entire territory and plot reasonable destinations and routes. It is also a *way* of looking at the territory, through certain lenses. On a backpacking trip, for example, the macroview allows the hiking planner to see the boundaries of the wilderness region, the two or three major established trails that may exist in the area, the distance in miles (but not in perspiration or fatigue) between two points, and the valleys, rivers, meadows, and mountains that make up the area. It is only from this comprehensive picture of the terrain that the hiker can set overall goals for the trip. This is so because once on the forest trail, visibility is reduced to the bend ahead, and aspirations can be diverted by emotional and physical fatigue. Unexpected events like a blistered foot or temptations like an idyllic stream encountered near high noon can take the hiker off course. It is knowing the whole map that allows the traveler to flexibly engage with these distractions yet still achieve intended outcomes.

Like the hiker, presenters with conscious access to their macromaps can make decisions during the presentation that are congruently related to the large picture. They can seize opportunities, which would go unrecognized without the maps, to move a group toward envisioned destinations. What macromaps guide the design work of premier presenters? Three will be discussed here: (1) each audience contains four subaudiences, (2) learning

[1]I am particularly grateful to Suzanne Bailey of Bailey Alliance, Bill Baker of Group Dynamics Associates, Bruce Wellman of Science Resources, and Diane Zimmerman in the Davis School District for helping me with my thinking on this topic.

accelerates at higher levels on an intervention taxonomy, and (3) efficacy facilitates personalized learning, transfer, and application.

Presenters apply knowledge of these maps by speaking to four audiences to get their message heard and learned, leveraging presentation time to transform the power of their work, and empowering audiences as the ongoing subtext of their message (see Figure 1.2).

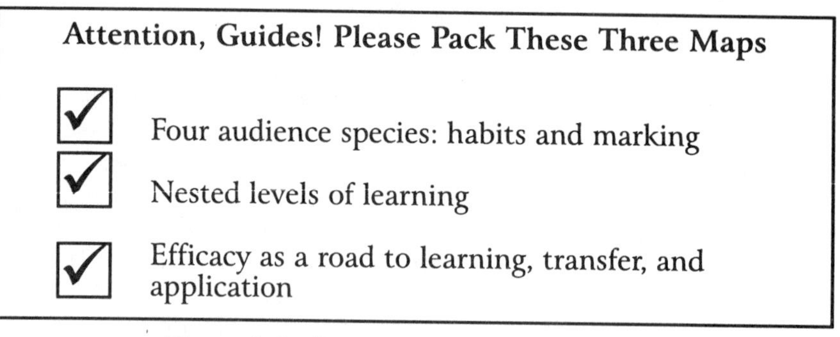

Figure 1.2: Presenters Use Three Maps

Speak to Four Audiences

I once watched a performer in a Beirut nightclub present to an audience whose members spoke Arabic, French, or English. Like the carnival performer who spins a series of plates on sticks, this trilingual performer balanced his time in the three languages, being careful not to spend too much time in, for example, French, because the English and Arabic speakers might feel left out and grow bored.

In a similar manner, because of audience learning style preferences and variations in the ways in which people take in and process information, premier presenters target four different audiences in each presentation.

The presenter designs each session, and each segment within a session, to attend to four audience types: the "professors," the "friends," the "inventors," and the "scientists." As shown in Figure 1.3, these groups are primarily concerned with answering different questions: *what, so what, what if,* and *why.*

- **What?**
  The *professors* value data and expect the presenter to be an authority. They appreciate handouts, bibliographies, a sequentially arranged agenda, and structure. Seating arrangements that signal a lecture are pleasing.

These people want mastery and competence. They want to be able to **remember** the information and to perform the skills that are presented.

Professors

Presentation Tips

Provide facts, lecture, citations, quotes, examples, demonstrations, practice, feedback, drill, sequence, detail, overt organization, and a detailed bibliography.

Engage them with Facts

So what ?

These people want involvement and engagement with other participants. They want to **respond** to the topic through interpersonal relations. Feeling tone is important to them.

Friends

Presentation Tips

Provide emotional hooks, personal stories, metaphors, inventories, opportunities for sharing, choosing and relating the topic to oneself and others through hands-on and group activities.

Attend to their Feelings

Speaking to Four Audiences

These people want to under-stand and comprehend. They want to **reason** with the information that is being presented.

Scientists

Presentation Tips

Provide concepts, ideas, data, opportunities to examine and process the data, formulate explanations, make judgments, and inquire. They like structure and organization.

Involve them in Formulating Ideas

What if?

These people want to adapt, modify, extend, explore, and create. They want to **reorganize** the information into new and different arrangements.

Inventors

Presentation Tips

Provide opportunities for creative self-expression, and individual and group exploration, where they can reorganize what is known to make new connections and original creations.

Take them on Flights of fantasy

Adapted from the "Thoughtful Education Model" developed by Hanson, Silver Strong Associates, Morristown, NJ.

Figure 1.3: Speaking to Four Audiences

- **So what?**
  The *friends* may enjoy entering a room with round tables or seating in a circle because these signal that interaction will occur in the session. They will appreciate an opening mixer that allows them to meet others and will probably value wearing name tags.
- **What if?**
  The *inventors* may appreciate an agenda displayed as a mind map (even though this may drive some professors crazy). They enjoy colorful charts and synectic exercises, particularly as openings. Synectics involves a small group using metaphor or analogy to state or solve a problem. For example, a small group might answer the question, "Restructuring schools is like what sporting event—and why?"
- **Why?**
  The *scientists* will value agendas that are organized around questions central to the topic and handouts that provide space for reflection and inquiry.

Skilled presenters warm the stage for each of these audiences prior to a presentation and attend to these four styles within the opening minutes and throughout the presentation. They may do this at first by informally saying hello to participants before the presentation begins and by including in the opening a *brief* self-introduction that establishes the presenter's "credentials" on this topic, a relevant story, a few figures or facts, and an opportunity for participants to buzz with one another. (See the section on indirect stories in Chapter 4 for some tips on which types of stories are most appreciated by each of these four audiences.) Within the space of a few minutes, the presenter has connected with each of the audience styles. Unless one is presenting to a highly specific subset of the profession, such as technology experts or drama teachers, most audiences will be mixed, and a skilled presenter will watch carefully to maintain a balance throughout the rest of the presentation. After a session, they read the evaluations to learn which groups they served well and which felt unattended. Not surprisingly, presenters tend to do best with audience members most like themselves and are least effective with the group least like themselves. Taken in this light, the participant evaluations become a valuable self-coaching tool.

Amplify Presentations by Working at Strategically Selected Levels of Intervention

Just as presenters work with taxonomies of both the cognitive and affective domains, they also apply a taxonomy of intervention, seeking to direct training energies to the levels that will produce the most growth. At the lowest end of this continuum are presentations that work to change or improve specific behaviors; the next level is capabilities, followed by beliefs, and, finally, identity. I will elaborate on each of these (see Figure 1.4).

- **Behaviors**
  Identifying characteristics of at-risk children, distributing student response opportunities more equitably, becoming a better paraphraser, identifying a dependent clause, and learning to wait after asking students a question are all examples of behavioral-level training objectives. Presentation goals at this level are low on Bloom's Taxonomy of The Cognitive Domain and are expressed as the attainment of knowledge or skills. They contribute least to transformational growth.

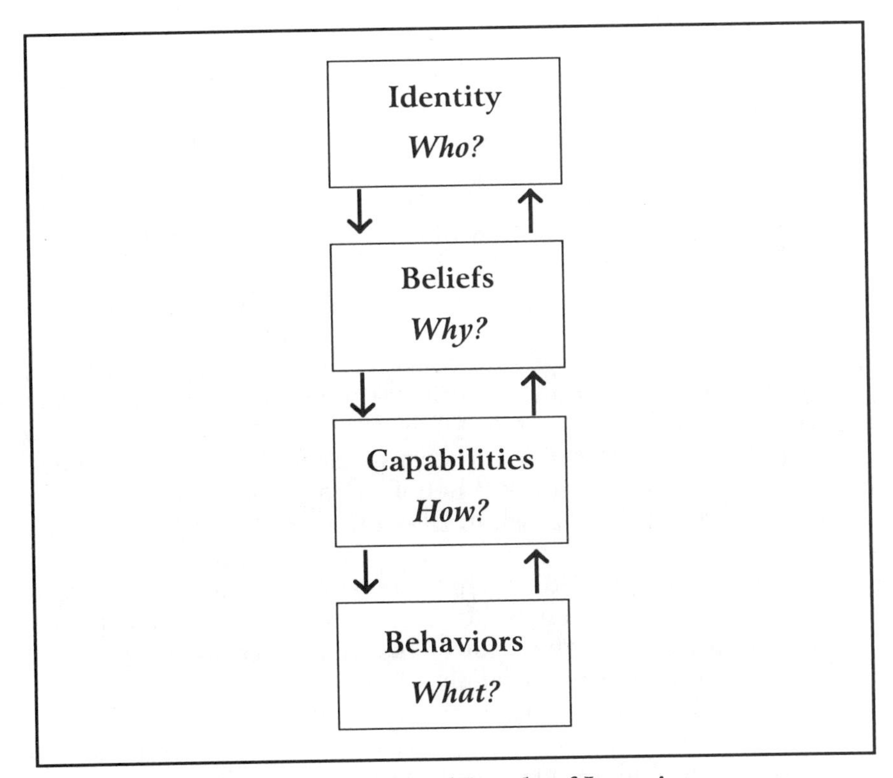

Figure 1.4: Logical Levels of Learning

Adapted from R. Dilts' "'Nested' Levels of Experience," 1994.

- **Capabilities**
These have to do with the mental strategies and maps that the participants develop to guide their specific behaviors. These cognitive strategies help participants determine when certain behaviors are appropriate and help them invent new behaviors to accomplish their goals. Interventions at participants' levels of capacities contribute to the achievement of clusters of behaviors rather than just single behaviors. The degree to which group members are able to generalize something to new situations outside of the training context is a function of their attainment at this level of the intervention taxonomy.
- **Beliefs**
This level of intervention has to do with participants' values and belief systems. Values are our internal guidelines for what is good, bad, worthy, or unworthy. Beliefs are ideas or concepts that we hold to be true. In addition to developing behavioral skills and capabilities, a training program must also address the presuppositions, beliefs, and values of the participants. The way in which some learning fits (or does not fit) into the personal or cultural value systems of the individual or group will determine how it will be received and incorporated.

    Beliefs primarily concern the permission that participants grant themselves to engage in new behaviors. For example, a teacher who begins to believe that students can learn more by working together than alone will be motivated to learn and apply the ideas and skills related to cooperative learning. When presenters engage participants in exploring their beliefs related to a topic, when they use metaphors to indirectly suggest a topic-appropriate useful belief structure, when they offer data that supports a belief in a practice—say cooperative learning, and when they invite participants to examine situations from the perspectives of others, they are intervening at the level of beliefs. Presenters also intervene at the level of beliefs when they offer opportunities for participants to challenge their assumptions and their understanding of a topic. All learners come to the learning situation with preconceived beliefs. My friend Laura Lipton tells about a kindergarten child who reported that red leaves are heavier than green ones because they fall first from the tree! Since we tend to take in all new information in ways that make it reinforce current understandings, some of these prior understandings will enhance further learning, and some will interfere.

An excellent film that demonstrates this phenomenon is *Project Star: A Private Universe*, (1992). Harvard graduates were interviewed on their graduation day on the subject, "What causes the seasons?" Of about twenty-four people interviewed (including a science major), only one was able to answer the question correctly. For these bright and educated people, early misunderstandings about the tilt of earth as it orbits the sun, varying distances between earth and sun, and other ideas had dominated and shaped all new information they had learned on this topic. Interventions at the level of values and beliefs provoke greater changes than training directed at either the levels of capabilities or behaviors.

- **Identity**
  The identity level involves the sense of self that is experienced by the group or group members. Identity issues are at the core of who we think we are. All our perceptions of ourselves, others, and the environment flow from this sense of identity. Ultimately, all beliefs, capabilities, and behaviors are rooted in identity. Because of this, change at this level will often reverberate to other levels. Psychologist Michael Brickey (1991) comments, "I am impressed that often the most elegant, quick, and lasting changes take place at the identity level."

  Identity influences incorporation of information at the deepest levels, participants' responsibility for what was learned, and commitment to putting it into action. Identity shapes the perceived mission of each person and group. Approaches that affect identity include the construction of metaphor that can lead groups to new conceptions of self, experiences in which participants discover a portion of themselves not previously acknowledged, workshop practices that shift the spotlight from the presenter as an information dispenser to participants as knowledge constructors, and the pursuit of empowerment outcomes in the presentation.

Transformational presentations regard these levels of intervention as "nested;" that is, influencing one level will automatically modify the levels below. Transformational presenters also ask themselves, "How can I teach behaviors in ways which can affect capabilities, beliefs, and identity?"

Empower the Audience

To *feel* empowered is the first step in *being* empowered. The best presenters consistently aim to assist audiences in reaching this state. Perception shapes reality; this is a rich example of cause and effect. Central to being empowered is a sense of efficacy. This state of mind contributes to a sense of personal identity that is capable of taking charge and producing results.

Efficacy means feeling that one makes a difference. To be efficacious is to regard oneself as the driver rather than the passenger in life. Efficacious teachers work harder than their lower-efficacy colleagues. They are more successful and they persevere through difficulties. They seek to understand multiple causes for instructional problems, come up with alternative solutions, and find the resources necessary to take action. Interestingly, efficacious teachers also experience less stress than more externally controlled teachers (see Figure 1.5).

Empowered staffs feel efficacious. They feel that their ideas are listened to, that their energies make a difference, and that it is worthwhile for them to contribute to the organization because something happens as a result of their participation. They pose questions and search for problems to solve. They are optimistic, self-actualizing, self-modifying, and able to invent new practices that they can translate into deliberate actions. One major value of efficacy is that it frees up common sense. The more efficacy one feels, the more flexibility can safely be engaged. In the Rand Corporation's seminal research on school improvement efforts, Paul Berman and Milbrey McLaughlin (1980) found that this sense of efficacy was the single most consistent variable for schools that were successful at meeting program objectives and attaining long-range changes in teacher behaviors.

When teachers are efficacious, they

- work harder than when they are not
- are more successful
- experience less stress
- are optimistic
- display more common sense
- are more flexible
- have students who learn more and are more cooperative

Figure 1.5: Benefits of Efficacy

Presenters fan the embers of efficacy with a number of subtle moves. They provide choice: where to sit, how long the break should be, what personal goals to work on, whom to pick as partner, how to approach a small group task, and which homework suggestions to pursue. Presenters also consistently use language that presupposes the existence of a state of efficacy: "As you decide what's most important to you...," "As you tell others what you have learned from this day...," "As you recall previous successes...," "Knowing that you are busy people and that you intend to produce as much value for yourself as possible today...," "As you examine your strengths...."

Efficacy is enhanced when participants help shape agendas to their needs, when they teach others, when they control their own learning goals and environment, and when they look at their own behavior from the perspective of choice. Presenters promote this viewpoint when they respond to statements such as, "There's just too much to cover, and not enough time" with language that reminds the participants that, despite existing environmental constraints, they always maintain choice; for example, "So you're in the process of deciding which portions of the curriculum are most important for your students."

Because educational goals are achieved through groups of people, it makes sense to speak to each person in the way that allows him or her to learn best; to promote awareness of personal identities that are caring, collaborative, and successful; and to continually shape efficacy in ourselves, our audiences and our students. It is the hiker who knows he or she can complete the journey, who does so; it is the traveler who knows the territory who attains the outcome and enjoys the trip.

Your Presentation Is a Gift

How can a presentation be like a gift? This is an important achievement in presentations that seek to transform, because gifts bring an audience and presenter together in special ways. A relationship emerges in which personalization, caring, and lightness prevail, and in which the audience is signaled, "I know who you are, I care for you, and I have selected something specifically for you."

I learned this concept first from working with John Grinder of Grinder, DeLozier Associates, and later from watching and working with presentation virtuoso Suzanne Bailey (Garmston and Bailey, 1988). I've learned to apply this concept in practical ways during a presentation or workshop.

In the verb "to present" lives the inference that three entities exist: (1) a presenter (one who presents), (2) a present(ation) (that which is being presented), and, (3) a presentee (the receiver). A presenter, then, is one who brings a gift.

Consider the attributes of an exemplary presentation. It is personal, selected specifically for you; it is communicated about and perhaps received within an aura of suspense; it is attractively wrapped; and it is useful.

The Best Gifts Are Personal

Consider a few of the best gifts you have received. It's likely that in each case, regardless of cost, it was special because it was something picked exclusively with you in mind; not just any blouse or shirt, cologne, or card, but one that's "you," specially suited to your interests and tastes. This first attribute is related to the three rules for effective presenting, as espoused by Walter Cronkite and other authorities: (1) Know your audience! (2) Know your audience! (3) Know your audience! Presenters who apply this first attribute customize presentations for the specific audience they are addressing. To customize, of course, requires knowledge about the group. With just a little effort, you can do the research necessary to personalize your presentation through customizing your comments about the time, the place, the circumstances, or yourself.

Figure 1.6 shows four examples of customizing comments that do not take a lot of preparation. Of course, anything you say to personalize your presentation must convey respect for the audience. An attorney once opened a presentation to teachers by saying, "I always wanted to be a teacher." Now, that seems like a good start in making a connection with the audience, doesn't it? "But," the speaker went on to say, "when I found out how much money teachers make and how much attorneys make, I changed my mind." That comment also changed the rapport that was beginning to build with the audience—for the worse. This is not the kind of personal reference you want to use.

You can also make a presentation personal by investing a bit more research time into who the group is and what they are about before you present. Requesting copies of newsletters, staff memos, mission statements, or statements of practice or policy can give you a deeper understanding of the values, events, and

Quick-Prep Steps to Customize Your Presentation

1. **The time.** During your opening comments, refer to the time, date, holiday, or significance of this time for this topic. *"It's appropriate that we be gathered here for this topic on the eve of celebrating Martin Luther King Day."*
2. **The place.** Mention the location in which you are working to establish a common reference with the group. *"Today we meet in this room called a Learning Center, surrounded by books and technology. But if this is the Learning Center of the school, then what are the classrooms? You and I know that the learning that occurs in your classroom each day through your interaction with students is the learning that counts most. That is the learning we will address today."*
3. **The circumstances.** Comment about a current item in the news. Make reference to the setting: it's hot, cold, crowded, or snowing, or report cards have just been issued. For example, when in Chicago you can say, *"What about those Bulls in last night's game!?"*
4. **Yourself.** Use something unique about yourself as a point of reference. *"I like to hike and whenever I can I will go into the mountains for a few days with a friend, a backpack, and a good map. On my last trip something happened that comes to mind whenever I think of today's topic."*

Figure 1.6: Customize Your Presentation

Adapted from J. Cathcart, 1995

issues important to the group. Coming early and getting to know representative members of the group allows you to refer to them in your presentation. "As Sarah would probably tell you...," or, "When I was talking with several members of the science department earlier I learned that..." Statements of acknowledgment, when sincere, are also appreciated and help connect you with the audience: "...and in this district where you enjoy such an excellent reputation for leadership..."

Stir in Some Suspense

A second characteristic of a great gift is that it's cloaked with suspense. Remember birthdays as a child—the waiting, the curiosity, the urge to peek? Presenters create some of this same anticipation in opening remarks: "Later I will describe a special gift I think you'll find useful..."; or in the overview: "We'll conclude by reporting the findings on topic X, some of which you may find surprising." This foreshadowing can activate some of the curious child in audience members.

Wrap It in Beautiful Paper

A third characteristic of an appreciated gift is that it is attractively wrapped. Carefully designed handouts send a signal that you care enough to send the very best. Arranging the room for comfort and easy visibility and hearing wraps you and your message nicely. Your own dress is important. For an excellent source on choosing the right clothes for presentation, see Ian Ewing's *The Best Presentation Skills.*

Presentation wrapping might also include artful phrasing, surprising sequence, a public agenda posted on chart paper, food (in the "Audience Rapport section of Chapter 3 I'll report on research linking food to audience approval of ideas!), or even a bit of drama. Notice the "meaning last" sequence in this next sentence. "The passenger next to me was an off-duty pilot hitching a ride to St. Louis. I thought about the stereotype we have of pilots: tall, good looking, bronzed face, easy grin. This one was no exception. 'Cockpit management and an emphasis on the interpersonal skills of leading a crew is now the rage in pilot in-service training,' she said."

Make It Useful

Finally, and perhaps most important, an appreciated gift is more than aesthetic, it is something that you will want to use. I've found it helpful to suggest uses for elements that I am teaching in several contexts. In Chapter 3, a section on Triple Track

Presenting offers some specific strategies to help participants transfer what they've learned in a variety of ways. Again, the adage "know your audience" prevails and guides' a presenter in a careful balance between theory and practice. This leads some presenters to be called "amphibians": those who are easily at home with the theory of things and who can also explain the day-to-day nuts and bolts of implementation.

Presenting to Groups Experiencing Change

Notes from a Safari Journal

The African elephant is as big as a truck, with a nose as long as its legs. The trunk functions as a siphon, snorkel, squirt gun, trumpet, and feeding tool powerful enough to rip branches from trees but delicate enough, with fingerlike projections at the tip, to pick up a pea.

For centuries the elephants conducted an annual migration from the Serengeti—which in the language of the Masai means "endless plain"—to the Ngorongoro Crater, a water- and vegetation-rich haven. But less than a hundred years ago, farmers planted corn and potatoes in the sweeping hills between the plains and the crater, and the migrations stopped. Today, of the elephant family, only a few resident bull elephants graze at the bottom of the crater.

I recently worked with members of an organization in which catastrophic changes were occurring. Many had lost their jobs as a result of declining resources, and more positions were sure to go, but nobody knew which ones. The management team was struggling to implement a new strategic plan and introduce team building and participatory decision making into this formerly compartmentalized and top-down organization. Uncertainty and suspicion abounded, and many employees felt as if they were in the position of turkeys being asked to vote on Thanksgiving.

It was at this time that two gifts were given to me. First was a realization that, whatever the nature of the organization's agenda, the *people* were undergoing extreme stress and uncertainty. For the organization's goals to be achieved, personal anxieties needed to be addressed. Secondly, colleague and change-consultant extraordinaire Suzanne Bailey placed two books in my hands by William Bridges that spoke specifically to helping ourselves and others deal with transitions (Bridges, 1980, 1991). I began to ponder how a presenter, either internal or external to an organization, might make use of this knowledge to support people and organizations in high states of transition. The following are some thoughts on this matter.

It's not the changes in life that are difficult to deal with, observes Bridges; it's the transition periods, the natural processes of disorientation and reorientation that accompany them (Bridges, 1980). He describes these as *endings, neutral zones,* and *new beginnings.* For individuals to cope effectively with these stages, it's useful to know what they are and to have ideas on how to deal with them. People make new beginnings, says Bridges, only if they have first made an ending and spent some time in a neutral zone. But most presentations focus on the beginnings. Presenters can give a valuable gift to audiences when they learn enough about the organization to know in what stages of transition the people in it might be, and then organize their messages and learning experiences congruently with these transition zones.

Endings

Every transition, even from a joyous event, starts with an ending. For the young couple welcoming a new baby in the house, there are still the endings: of a full night's sleep, of private time for the couple, of extra money. In schools, a new program or curriculum, no matter how positively anticipated, brings an ending to the old ways of doing things: the familiarity of texts and exercises, instructional strategies, patterns of relationships with other adults, perhaps even changes in status.

During this period it is normal to feel a sense of loss, even grieving, for the old. It is sometimes a slow process, for we may have identified some portion of who we are with what is past. It is a time in which we may feel disoriented, disenchanted, angry, or depressed. Since the biggest task each person faces during an ending is to let go of what is passing, perhaps the most important service that staff developers can do is to let others react to the ending. Endings are, after all, experiences of dying, and in some sense we may feel that they may mean the end of us. Yet our logical minds know that an ending marks the beginning of a new life.

Tips for Presenters Working with Groups at Endings

Expect and accept some signs of grieving. People may be sad, angry, depressed, nonrational, frightened, or confused. Take these as signs of coping with loss, not as bad morale. What you can offer participants at this stage is a nonjudgmental atmosphere and a process through which feelings can be expressed. For example, have people in pairs list all the "losses" involved in a change, or have small groups list the worst things, the best things, and the most probable things that might happen in relation to a new program. Have people talk about their feelings. Have groups respond to prompts such as, "Working with the new program is like what household object, because..."

The trick in endings is to let go. Prepare yourself for presentations by thinking about who in the organization will be losing what in the change. Think and feel from their perspective. The loss of comfort, confidence, routines, security, relationships, status, and years of "being effective doing it this way" may be involved. Is there something that's over for everyone? Perhaps a chapter is over in the school's history. Perhaps the school is experiencing loss of significant personnel or declining enrollment or changes in demographics. Tell stories that legitimize participants' uncomfortable feelings with endings and stories that signal the transitions to follow.

To help people let go, include in your presentation information about transitions. Put more energy into explaining the circumstances that led to the change and less energy into the solutions. We typically try to "sell" the solutions, says Bridges, before the problems that necessitated the changes are fully understood and accepted. Identify the specific behaviors that participants will need to be able to accomplish the change. Be explicit about them and teach them. Give people information about the change. Update the data. You cannot communicate too much. My friend Michael Buckley, whose drawings you see in this book, says we must "overcommunicate." Finally, treat the past with respect. Frame whatever is passing as useful to what you are moving toward. Remember that people may identify with past practices in a positive way. Never, never, demean the old way of doing things.

The Neutral Zone

Bridges calls this state the neutral zone because it is a "nowhere between two somewheres" (Bridges, 1991). In organizations, anxiety rises and motivation falls. Performance declines and the number of missed workdays increases. People get overloaded, signals are mixed, systems are in flux, and more things go wrong. In significant life transitions, people often intuitively seek solitude to sort things out. The critical task at this stage is to give in to the emptiness that one is experiencing and trust that a death-and-rebirth process is in progress. It is this very process of disintegration and reintegration that becomes the source of renewal.

Tips for Presenters Working with Groups at the Neutral Zone

The first order of business is to take care of yourself. To get in touch with what it's like to be in the neutral zone during your own transition, and to get maximum benefit, try these ideas. Find a regular time to be alone, even if it is as simple as rising half an hour earlier each day to have a cup of coffee and reflect. Develop a journal of your own journey through the neutral zone. What are you thinking and feeling? What new awarenesses about yourself are you developing? This can be a rich period of personal discovery and creativity. Take advantage of it. Arrange a few days' "passage journey" for yourself in which you are alone in a new setting without distractions. Provide a holiday for the mind and soul, as it were, and a chance for the processes of reintegration to take place.

In your presentations, normalize the neutral zone. Forecast its occurrence, processes, and benefits. Select metaphors with positive attributes to describe the changes that people are experiencing. Instead of a "sinking ship," speak of the ship's new route. (This presumes a destination, a new port, possibly a retrofitting.) Use metaphors of life cycles, seasons, and growing things to talk about the changes.

Stimulate ideas. Frame problems as entryways to new solutions. Get people brainstorming, sharing, and envisioning. Because the neutral zone is the place of new growth, work to get as many ideas out in the open as possible. Let people know that the neutral zone is the best place to generate and test new ideas and that innovation will take place naturally if they seed the ground with lots of thoughts.

Work to strengthen each person's sense of interdependence. Use presentation strategies that involve group problem finding and solution sharing. Interdependence is an essential state of mind for schools in transition. Susan Rosenholtz (1989), in her study of elementary schools in Tennessee, found that the single most important characteristic of successful schools was goal consensus. Jon Saphier, of Research for Better Teaching, reports that the issue of good schools is so simple that it's embarrassing: People have common goals and work together toward those goals.

People who are interdependent seek collegiality and give of themselves to group goals and needs. They feel a sense of community. They ask for help and they give help. Just as they contribute to a common good, they also draw on the resources of others. Anything that presenters do to enhance the skills and attitudes of interdependence supports a group in moving healthily through the neutral zone, and in fact is a potent resource for dealing with the new beginning.

New Beginnings

Genuine beginnings start within us. They are psychological phenomena that we come to, paradoxically, only at the end of something else. This is the time for action and the pursuance, step by step, of a plan to take us to the new place.

Tips for Presenters Working with Groups at New Beginnings

Focus participants on the processes that will lead to outcomes, not the outcomes themselves. Foreshadow for people the normal brief decline in effectiveness when working with any new strategy. As learners move through the stages of *unconscious incompetence* (I don't know that I don't know) to *conscious incompetence* (I know that I don't know) to *conscious competence,* they often expect the effortlessness that comes only at the later stage of *unconscious competence* (I know it as well as my own name and so I don't have to put conscious effort into it). By alerting people to the effort required in the conscious competence stage, you encourage them to not abandon ship during the rough seas, so they can stay on board for the smooth sailing that is sure to come.

Be clear with people about the purpose for the new beginning and support them in identifying themselves with the final result. Offer precise pictures of what staff and students will be saying, doing, and feeling once the change is complete. Invite them to help construct images of the desired state. Do not, however, build a picture of the future so complicated and far removed from existing realities that people feel overwhelmed and intimidated with the task.

Finally, monitor yourself for what Bridges calls the *marathon effect*. Often speakers on change have already gone through the three stages of transition themselves before they make presentations to others. They are like professional athletes in a public marathon. Hundreds of people are lined up, scores deep at the starting line. The race begins, but the occasional runners, those at the very end of the pack, don't actually cross the starting line until the ones in the lead have already settled into their stride. After a while, the front runners are thinking about the end of the race and the next challenge. In that moving mass of runners, however, there are still many just dealing with starting.

Once, in a race that my wife and I experienced, friends would periodically join a runner, run alongside to pace that individual, and offer encouragement. The best presentations will do that verbally for each member of the audience, regardless of which stage of the race they are in at the moment.

End Notes

Berman, P. & McLaughlin, M. (1980). Factors affecting the process of change. In M. Milstein (ed.), *Schools, Conflicts and Change*. New York: Teachers College Press.

Brickey, M. (1991). Making changes by changing identity. *Anchor Point* 5(11): 1–4.

Bridges, W. (1980). *Transitions: Making Sense of Life's Changes*. New York: Addison-Wesley.

Bridges, W. (1991). *Managing Transitions: Making the Most of Change*. New York: Addison-Wesley.

Cathcart, J. (1995). Customize your style and content to fit your audience. In Members of Speakers' Roundtable (eds.), *Speaking Secrets of the Masters: The Speakers' Roundtable*. Harrisburg, PA: Executive Books.

Costa, A. (1991). The school as a home for the mind. In A. Costa (ed.), *Developing Minds: A Resource Book for Teaching Thinking*. Alexandria, VA: Association for Supervision and Curriculum Development.

Costa, A. & Garmston, R. (1994). *Cognitive Coaching: A Foundation for Renaissance Schools*. Norwood, MA: Christopher-Gordon Publishers, Inc.

Costa, A. & Garmston, R. (In press). Maturing outcomes. *Educational Leadership*.

Dilts, R.B. (1994). *Effective Presentation Skills*. Capitola, CA: Meta Publications.

Elmore, R.F. (1995). Structural reform and educational practice. *Educational Researcher* 24(9): 23–26.

Elmore, R.F. & Fuhrman, S.H. (eds.). (1994). *The Governance of Curriculum: The 1994 ASCD Yearbook*. Alexandria, VA: Association for Supervision and Curriculum Development.

Fullan, M. (1993). *Change Forces: Probing the Depths of Educational Reform*. Bristol, PA: Falmer Press.

Garmston, R. & Bailey, S. (1988). Paddling together: A copresenting primer. *Training and Development Journal* 42(1): 52–57.

Jaccaci, A.T. (1989). The social architecture of a learning culture. *Training and Development Journal* 43(11): 50–53

Joyce, B. & Showers, B. (1988). *Student Achievement through Staff Development*. New York: Longman.

Kegan, R. (1982). *The Evolving Self: Problem and Process in Human Development*. Cambridge, MA: Harvard University Press.

Pedersen, D. (1990). Unpublished Manuscript. Sacramento, CA: California State University.

Pyramid Film & Video (producer). (1992). *Project Star: A Private Universe*. Santa Monica, CA: Pyramid Film & Video.

Rosenholtz, S.S. (1989). *Teachers' Workplace: The Social Organization of Schools*. New York: Longman.

Saphier, J. & Gower, R. (1987). *The Skillful Teacher: Building Your Teaching Skills*. Carlisle, MA: Research for Better Teaching, Inc.

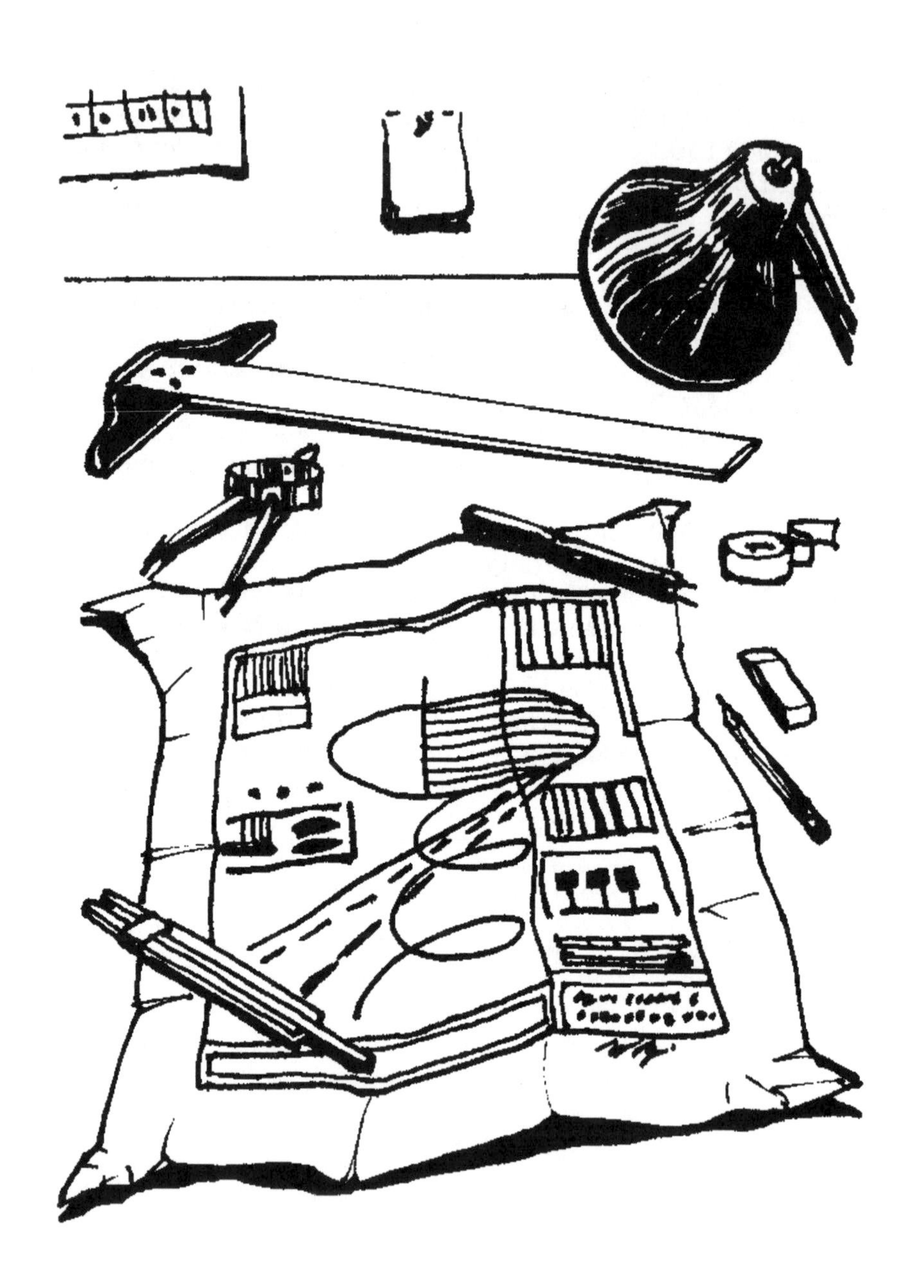

CHAPTER 2 How to Design Effective Presentations

Make your plans big enough to include God and large enough to include eternity.

Martin Luther King, Jr.

A guide must equip oneself with many maps of the territory. As described in Chapter 1, some of these relate to presentations designed to transform, some help one to select the most potent learning outcomes from those possible for both the short and long range, some relate to supporting people through the psychological transitions associated with any change, and others deal with customizing a presentation to the audience type.

The good guide designs a journey by using these maps but also uses navigational aids of greater detail and specificity to the presentation itself. Among these are charts that outline the steps to take before a presentation, plots on which content selections can be made, an outline of the tensions represented by getting the right process-content ratios, ways to plan for collaboration, and organizers for brief sorties into special areas.

 *Notes from a Safari Journal*

I notice that Juma has a stack of books in the space between the driver's seat and the passenger's seat. Occasionally he will stop the Land Rover, reach for his binoculars, then refer to one of his reference books. "That's a reichenow weaver," he says, pointing to a yellow-eyed bird with a black ear patch encircled with yellow and a bright yellow forecrown. "It's a small finchlike bird with a pointed beak that is good for eating seeds of grasses, buds, and insects. Look, there may be its nest!" Amazed, we follow his direction to see dozens of round yellow straw-bag nests hanging from branches like ornaments on a Christmas tree.

Before the Opening

A late flight leads to an unscheduled overnight stay in a connecting city. My luggage catches up with me the next morning as I disembark in the city in which I am to present. The session is scheduled to start at 9:00 A.M. I arrive at 8:55 A.M. after a frantic taxi drive from the airport. My first hour lacks artistry, and it isn't until after the first break that I catch my psychological breath and can function with ease.

This all-too-real experience reinforced my awareness that attention to details before the opening adds elegance and focus to a presentation. For the presenter, getting there *on* time means getting there *before* time. Certain "before-the-opening" details, when unattended, allow problems to emerge. Because presenting is such a complex mental activity, speakers need to place 100 percent of their mental resources on what's most important—the audience's interaction with the content. The handling of minor decisions ("Where should I put the overhead pens?") draws important energies away from this task.

Prespeech jitters are amazingly common. While sitting on the dais, I have seen the hand wringing, trembling notes, and perspiration of well-known speakers. Experienced speakers anticipate this anxiety and increase their resourcefulness and effectiveness by settling certain presentation logistics before they begin.

They typically come early to do this. It's not unusual to see the most skilled speakers arrive a full hour prior to the presentation. Before the opening they attend to (1) the comfort and perspective of audience members, (2) the ambiance and utility of the presentation environment, and (3) the presenter's work space. (see Figure 2.1).

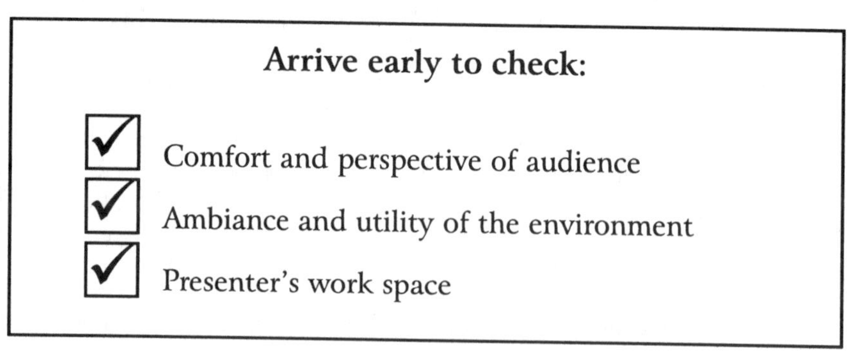

Figure 2.1: Before the Presentation

I have learned the following before-the-opening tips from experienced presenters.

Comfort and Perspective

- Walk around the room to observe what participants will be able to see from various seats. Sit. Imagine a head in front of you. Note how much of the projection screen or easel can be seen over that head. (Usually this is only the top two-thirds of the screen.) Put masking tape on the side of the overhead projector and/or easel to indicate visibility zones.
- Make a final check on refreshment arrangements. In the morning, fresh brewed caffeinated and decaffeinated coffee, fruit juice, hot water, tea, and chocolate drink packets are sound basics. When snacks are included, participants are increasingly desiring fruit in addition to or instead of pastries. Provide cold drinks in the afternoon.
- Establish a registration area with handouts, sign-in sheets (if required), and a person to welcome participants and answer questions. Provide preprinted name tags, or have a model name tag and instruct participants to complete theirs with felt-tip pens so that first names can be read twelve feet away. You'll want to call them by name without squinting.
- Plan to complete all before-the-opening preparations thirty minutes prior to your opening so that you can relax and personally greet participants; take this opportunity to learn about their interests, concerns, and experiences, and let them know something about you.

The Learning Environment

- Provide music to set a welcoming tone and invite relaxation. Music affects the emotions, brain waves, and the in-the-moment learning capacity. Baroque music, at sixty beats per minute, is often associated with programs of accelerated learning. Bach, Vivaldi, Corelli, and Handel are suggested by Doug McPhee (1992) in an article describing music in the classroom. More lively music is also useful, particularly at breaks. Most modest-sized cassette players will produce adequate volume when enhanced through a sound system.
- Use props to create visual focus and make an aesthetically pleasant stage environment. A drama teacher in St. Louis once taught me about this "warming the stage" approach. The presenter's props are platforms, easels, screens, stools, and chairs. Arrange these to define (put boundaries on) the presentation area. Use colorful graphics that welcome people, name the session,

and display a public agenda. (See "Presentation As Theatre" in Chapter 5 for more ideas.)

- Decide what your position should be in the room to give the majority of the audience the best visual access to you at the opening. Plan to be there and stand still (so they can take stock of you) for the first few minutes. If you have a platform, by all means use it for your opening.
- Test the overhead projector. The two most common problems are poor focus and burnt-out bulbs. Be sure you have a spare bulb.
- Check for ambient lighting when using an overhead. Close the drapes, turn off banks of lights, or reposition the screen, if necessary, to cut glare. Write notes to yourself on the cardboard overhead frames.
- Check the sou-ou-ound systems. Check the sound systems. Enough said?
- If your face is going to be projected on large screens in an auditorium while you speak, prepare the room by preparing for your face beforehand. Because any nervousness or uncertainty you feel will be projected on the big screen, you must overprepare. If you're introducing someone, you should be there long enough to get past your nervousness. Therefore, overmemorize your introduction. Then, when you're at the podium, look into the bright lights behind the camera where the audience is and smile. Raise your eyebrows. Those big screens magnify all tense expressions, note reading, and the loss of presence with the audience.
- Decide what seating arrangement best fits the room and your learning objectives (Smith, 1984). (See Figure 2.2.)

Theater Style

If your presentation will primarily be a lecture and your group size is more than fifty, consider using theater style because this provides the greatest number of seats in the smallest space. The lack of tables makes audience member interaction difficult, however.

Chevron

Consider this style for groups of thirty to fifty when you want to promote presenter-audience dialogue but limit full-group discussion. This adds the advantage of tables but loses floor space. Hotels and conference facilities often set up a variation of this called *classroom style*, in which the tables are not angled but squarely face the podium like desks in a formal classroom. I usually prefer chevron over the classroom style, since it is less formal and gives participants greater visual access to other members of the group. However, it takes up more space than classroom style.

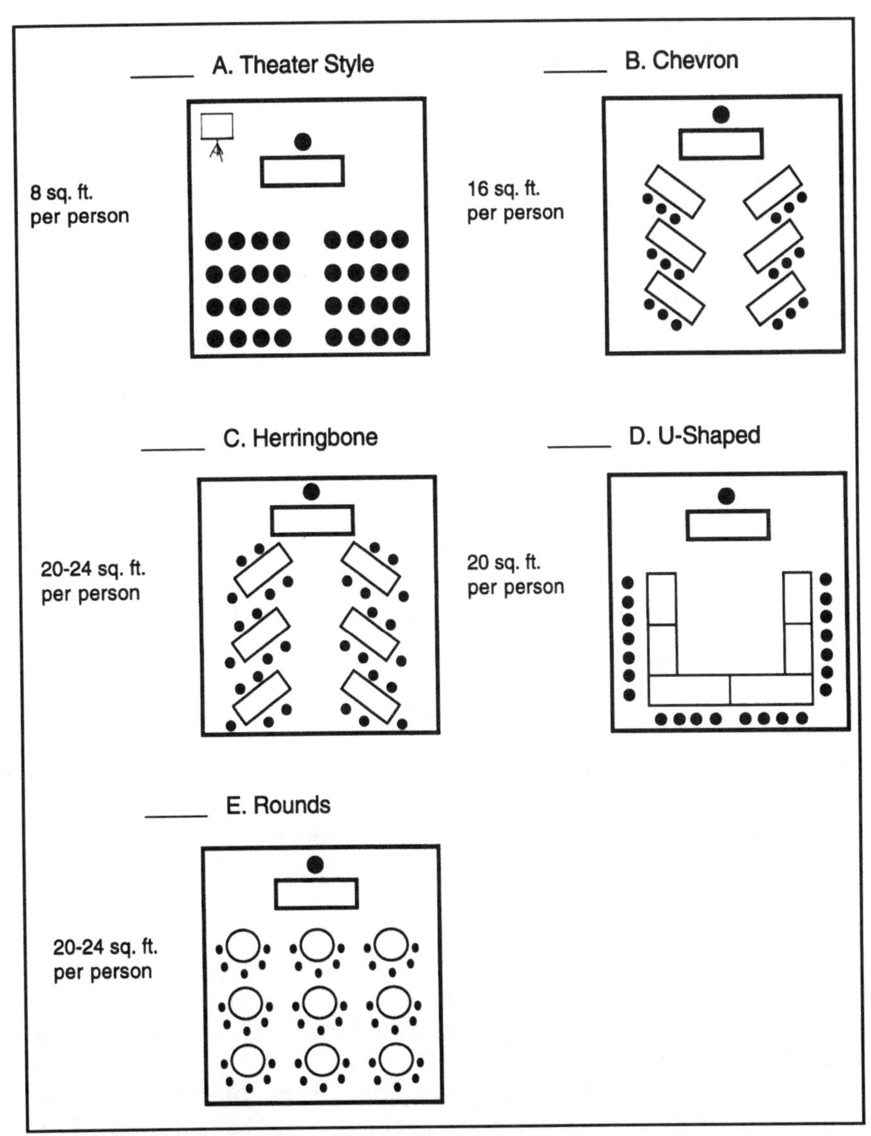

Figure 2.2: Room Arrangements

Herringbone

If your group size ranges from 30 to 150, use this alternative, which offers the advantages of classroom style to larger groups. In this arrangement, tables are angled so participants seated on both sides have either their right or left shoulders pointing toward the speaker. This allows for lecture-style learning *and* easy access to small-group discussions with people at the same table or different tables.

U-Shaped

If you want to signal equity in role and shared authority, use U-shaped seating for groups of fifteen to thirty in which each participant can see all others, thus promoting group dynamics. The presentation focus is the open end of the *U*. Use circled chairs or tables for a variation of this design for smaller groups (up to sixteen).

Rounds

Use rounds if your audience ranges in size from about 30 to 150 and you want participants to be actively engaged in learning activities a good deal of the time. From this arrangement, stable learning teams can be developed over full-day or multiday designs, yet enough flexibility exists to periodically assign participants across table groups for special activities. Seating participants in rounds facilitates group work and uses space, about twenty to twenty-four square feet per person. Both herringbone and rounds are supposed to take about an equal amount of space. In my experience, however, the rounds arrangement will typically seat a few more persons, regardless of the shape of the room.

The Presenter's Workspace

This final domain is largely about routinizing a number of logistical considerations, so that during the presentation your precious and limited mental space can be reserved for monitoring the audience's interaction with the content.

- Make final notes to yourself on your private agenda. Mark times in the margin to help you monitor and make adjustments as you present (see Figure 2.3).
- Stick one inch strips of masking tape along the side of the flip chart for quick paper hanging during the session. Having tape strips handy allows you to maintain presentation momentum. Consider using two flip charts to allow for more visual memory.
- Designate *a* space for pens, spare tape, blank overheads, and other needed items. Always return items to that spot. This is particularly important if you are presenting with a partner.
- Use *only* water-based felt-tip pens. They do not bleed through chart paper or make permanent marks on clothing, walls, or yourself. Use bright colors. While adequate pens can be found at Staples, Office Max, or other office supply stores, the very best pens are made by Paper Mate and are available through Interaction Associates (Attn: Howard Huberty, 600 Townsend St., Suite 550, San Francisco, CA 94103, 415–241–8000, fax 415–241–8010). They feature tips that hold up well over use and

a full range of bright colors: red, green, brown, blue, black, yellow, orange, and purple.

- Arrange two sets of transparencies. In one stack, place transparencies in the sequence in which you will use them. Arrange them in a binder, housed in translucent sleeves that can be placed directly on the overhead. This system allows for organization by category and easy reference to related

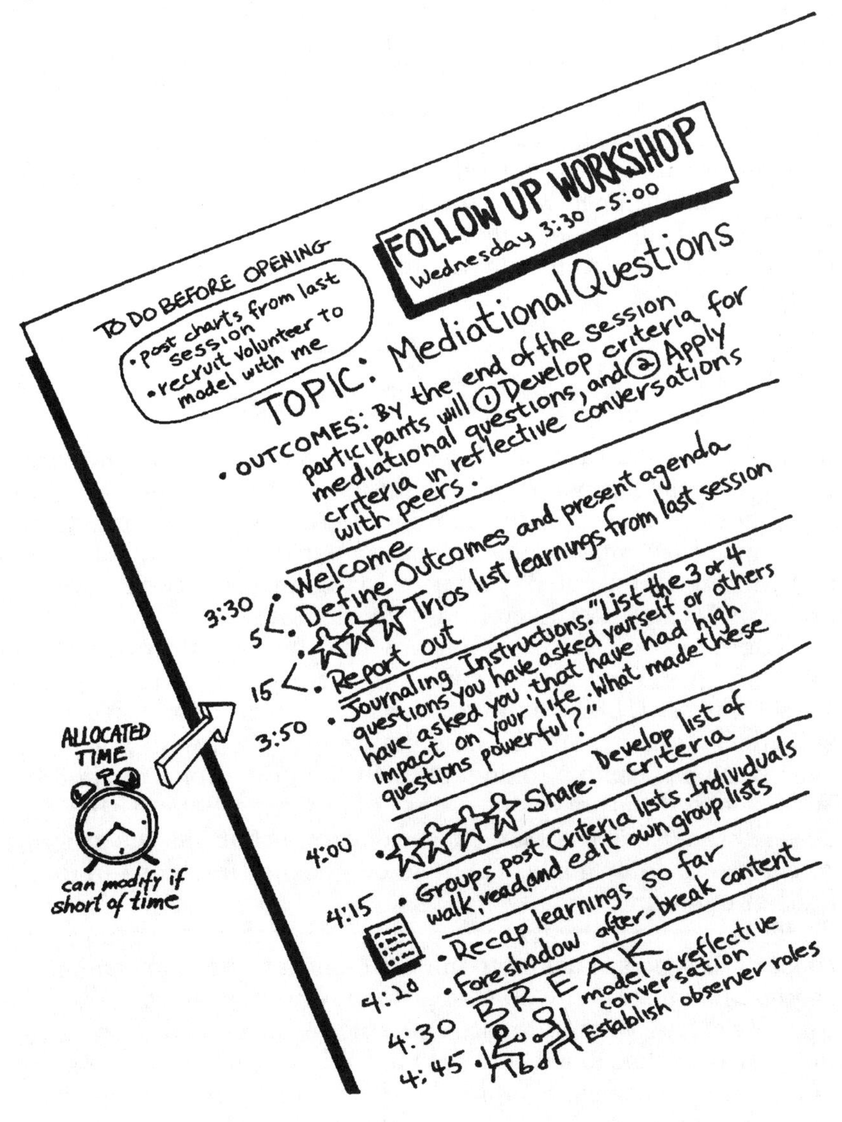

Figure 2.3: Presenter's Personal Agenda

transparencies that you may use on an occasional basis. Spread the second supplementary set out on a table to allow you to respond to the unique needs of the audience. Keep your visuals bold, colorful, and simple.

- If your session is going to be audiotaped, do a dry run to practice describing each visual that you use so the listening audience can derive maximum meaning.
- Declutter the entire presentation workspace environment. Remove briefcases, extra handouts, and *everything* you do not need to present your material. This eliminates visual distraction for the audience and mental distraction for you.
- Finally, place your private agenda at your fingertips so that you can unobtrusively refer to it at any time to stay on course.
- The audience will expect to be with you, each other, and the topic. All of these before-the-opening tasks make these expectations more attainable. Of course, it helps if your plane (and you) are on time.

Contracting a Presentation

Recently a consultant told me of this phone conversation with a school representative. "I'm calling to arrange for some staff development. We have six days and would like you to do one day on authentic assessment, one day on cooperative learning, one day on thinking skills, one day on peer coaching, one day on teaming, and one day on interdisciplinary curriculum."

There was a lo-o-ong silence while the consultant collected her thoughts. Finally she said, "I'm pleased for you that your school has been able to make such a significant commitment to staff development, and I'd be delighted to work with you. However, it is not possible to do justice to so many topics in six days. What I can do is to spend a day giving snapshots of these six areas and helping the staff choose one area that has the greatest relevance to their goals. Then we can design five days in depth on that one topic."

This incident illustrates a problem that is all too common to those of us who are asked to make presentations. Sometimes the request has not been well thought out, and if we do what we are initially asked, we may waste valuable resources. I say *resources,* not just *time,* because the most valuable resources are relationships and attitudes. Should these be damaged by inappropriately designed presentations, we have lost ground in the journey toward continuing school renewal.

I am fortunate to work frequently with many accomplished presenters, including Suzanne Bailey, Bill Baker, Art Costa, John Dyer, Laura Lipton, Peg Luidens, Marilyn Tabor, Bruce Wellman, and Diane Zimmerman. From these people I have learned the following about contracting for a presentation.

- You are a consultant before you are a presenter.
- Arrange a group contracting conversation.
- Work from a standard set of design questions.
- Work from a standard set of logistics questions.

You Are a Consultant Before You Are a Presenter

"Who am I" continues to be the most important design question and is especially relevant at this stage in your relationship with a client (Garmston and Wellman, 1992). Far from being just a hired mouth or an intelligent-looking face to fill an hour of time, you bring values and an expertise to the relationship that goes beyond your content knowledge. Once you are asked to present, you serve first as a consultant, a person whose expertise is used by others. Your role in the contracting dialogue is to be proactive, probing for the motivation behind the presentation request, pressing for precision in the description of outcomes, and being politely prescriptive (if your client hasn't considered it) about assessment and follow-up. Regardless of your work role—you are a teacher and the principal has asked you to present, or you are a staff developer and the superintendent wants a presentation to the board—remembering that you are first a consultant in this relationship will support you and the requesting party in creating the best possible presentation.

Arrange a Group Contracting Conversation

The person who contacts you for a presentation has *one* set of perceptions about what is needed. Several people will add dimensionality and richness and will increase the odds for a successful experience. I've learned to ask for either a face-to-face meeting or a group telephone call with four to eight persons representing different roles, levels, and perspectives within the group with which I'm being asked to work. Not only does this provide me with higher-quality data about the existing and desired conditions, it also provides local ownership for the presentation event. A forty-five-minute phone call is usually sufficient as long as I'm consciously working from the lists below. Some tips for group phone calls: Have a roster of names and ask people to name themselves before speaking. If you notice that someone is silent, you can ask for his or her reflections on what has been said so far. Have at least a verbal agenda so that you and the group can keep track of where you are. Reserve the right to limit decisions during the phone call to areas like outcome, audience, and logistics. Reserve final design rights to your deeper reflection.

Work from a Standard Set of Design Questions

I find it useful to work from the following list. By "work from," I do not mean that I use this as a sequential check list but rather as a reference document to remind me of particular areas that are useful to explore *in this conversation.*

- Is there a problem this event is intended to solve? If so, is training the best solution? Are there other solutions?
- Who is the audience? Are they volunteers? What are their roles? What are their attitudes about this topic, this presentation, or the work environment in general? What experiences, knowledge, skills, and potential contributions do they bring to this event?
- What are the outcomes? What will be seen, heard, or felt by the end of the presentation? What will be measurably different six weeks after the event? What is the connection between these outcomes and the long-term goals of the organization? What values will this event express and reinforce? In what ways will this event contribute to the states of mind of efficacy, interdependence, and consciousness?[2]

---

[2] See Fullan (1993) and Costa and Garmston (1994) for the importance of these states of mind. Fullan observes that the new problem in change is "...what would it take to make the educational system a learning organization—expert at dealing with change as a normal part of its work?" (p. 4). Educators, Fullan says, must see themselves and be seen as experts in the dynamics of change. He comments that to do this we must become inquirers and collaborators. If we do not achieve this, all we are doing is tinkering. Costa and Garmston describe cognitive coaching as the art of inquiry and illuminate how efficacy, interdependence, consciousness, and two other states of mind support collaboration, inquiry, change, and high performance, and how to coach for them.

- What is most important? Of all the possible outcomes, which are most critical? What *types* of outcomes are most desired—knowledge, skills, or attitudes?
- What follow-up support will be provided? What can be done to troubleshoot during implementation? What can be done to monitor for mutations—changes made during the application of learned skills that could either reduce or enhance their effectiveness? What can be done to personalize (individualize) follow-up? What data can be gathered with which to assess effects and design the next steps?
- What resources will we have to work with? How much time? Will there be a pre-event reading or dialogue? What syllabuses or readings should be provided at the event? What needs to be communicated to whom prior to the event?

Work from a Standard Set of Logistics Questions

- Might there be any surprises in the amount of actual presentation time? Can people *really* get back from lunch that soon? Will there be any business to conduct before this presentation starts?
- What physical setups are required?

  _____ name tags
  _____ audiovisual equipment
  _____ room arrangement
  _____ instructional materials
  _____ snack arrangements
  _____ participant groupings

- What travel and transportation details should we check? How do I get to your place and how long will it take me? Can I get in the room one hour before the event? Can someone help me transport materials and equipment?

In summary, presenters are consultants first, sharing their expertise and asking both design and logistics questions that are useful to the client. I encourage you to make your own set of contracting questions, tailored to your style and situation. And finally, two concluding tips: To paraphrase the advice of Publilius Syrus in 42 B.C., never promise more than you can perform. And to extend that advice from the perspective of staff development as we now envision it, never do only what is asked for, do what might be hoped for if it could be imagined.

Eight Design Questions for Self-Coaching

At my old school there is at least one teacher who loves me. She is the teacher who "knew me before I was born" and bought my first baby clothes. It is she who makes life bearable.

-Alice Walker,
In Search of Our Mothers' Gardens

I have the experience of traveling a lot and working in excellent districts with truly outstanding staff developers. In these settings I've watched skillful presenters orchestrate exceptional learning experiences in extraordinarily short periods of time. I've also seen some of my own relatively uninspired presentations produce magnificent learning because of the organizational culture and the receptivity of audiences. One result of these observations is that I have a renewed curiosity about the degree of my own effectiveness, and I am developing a new set of questions to guide my learning and growth.

These eight design and self-coaching questions are tightly interrelated and often seem to be different sides of the same coin. Each, however, offers a different perspective, and the eight, taken together, are contributing new insights and movement in my work. The questions seem to cluster around three themes:

1. Me, my practices, skills, routines, and approaches to presenting.
2. The audience, their perceptions of where they have been and are going, and the ultimate benefits they might derive from my work.
3. The future, the benefits and limitations of my own perceptual filters and mental models. How can I keep myself open to new and unexpected learning?

While the following questions are personal and will probably change because they reflect only my awareness of the moment, they may be illustrative to others in designing their own self-coaching guides.

Reflections about Me

- *What current practices can I discard to make room for new patterns in my work?*

  Like most persons who present frequently, over time I've developed some routines or approaches to particular topics. I keep using them because they are efficient (I don't need to keep inventing) and entertaining, they keep audiences engaged, and they quickly deliver information or skills. Now, however, I'm beginning to wonder *how much* learning is occurring with these techniques in which I've invested so heavily. Do I use them repeatedly primarily because they are easy? Are there other more powerful learning experiences that I might be providing? Are there different ways I might work? This leads to a related question.

- *What can I do to help audiences learn even more in the limited amount of time we have together?*

  I'm convinced that the best learning is more than just an engagement of the mind; it also comes from an affair of the heart and a connection with the community. In response to this second self-coaching question, I'm drawn to finding more and more ways to teach metaphorically. For example, in a recent training with Suzanne Bailey, at her suggestion we showed brief clips from *The Wizard of Oz* each day of the five-day workshop. While it's difficult to describe participant learning in behavioral terms, I "know" from watching the faces, and listening to people throughout the workshop, that very special and deep learning was taking place that could not have been achieved in more conventional ways. As a result, I am open to adding to my repertoire additional ways of using simulations, physical metaphors, songs, stories, and ways of putting audiences in charge of their own learning and producing their own knowledge.

- *Who am I ? Are my practices congruent with my values and beliefs?*

  When I pose this question I begin to examine the relationship between my behavior and my beliefs about adult learners; my view that learning should be joyous, practical, active, and personalized; the broader purposes of my work; generalizations about group dynamics; and ideas on organizational change. Indeed, I find the very process of externalizing these values and beliefs to be illuminating and helpful.

As Walt Disney has advised, when your values are clear, your decisions are easy.

- *Am I having fun?*

  Very early in my career, a mentor of mine advised me that if I wasn't having fun, I should change what I was doing. I have followed her advice (some say I haven't been able to hold a job), leaving positions when the excitement, challenge, or impact that I was creating began to be overshadowed by other factors. Today I realize how important it is to apply this question to my work as a guide in the arena of staff development, because a primary source of my own effectiveness is the energy, joy, and excitement I bring to the work.

Questions about the Audience

- *Who are they really and what do they want?*

  This question is causing me to refine my intelligence gathering processes prior to presentations and leading me to experiment with two prepresentation information-gathering phases. First is the contracting conversation, in which I learn about the leader's or leadership team's perception of the presentation goals and purposes; the knowledge, skills, and attitudes of the participants; and the environmental context for the work (see "Contracting a Presentation" in this chapter). The second phase is a presession survey of participants, in which I learn their perceptions of themselves in relationship to the topic. For example, I might ask, "If I were to survey your students about their impressions of you, what three words might I hear most often? Three years ago, how might their descriptions have been different? A year from now, what descriptions would you hope to hear?" I can also learn about participants' knowledge of the topic by asking them what personal rules or guidelines inform their work.

- *What outcomes, if achieved in this setting, would produce the greatest gain in capacity building for the group?*

  S. Covey (1989) identifies two persistent organizational goals. One is production and the second is production capability. I now regard the topic on which I've been asked to speak as the subgoal or "product" of the presentation. The more important goal is developing the production capability of the group. What might I do, while "producing," to illuminate and access the resources that are necessary to increase the group's capacity for facilitating its own learning, help people see beyond limiting paradigms, and enlist them in their own growth? Whenever I help people bring up the skills, knowledge, and emotions that are a prerequisite to success, support their development of interdependence, and help them to clarify their values, I make a major contribution to the larger goals of schooling and to the individual participants.

Questions about the future

Finally, I'm asking myself two questions to help me continue to grow in ways that I can't predict.

- *How can I force myself to operate out of my comfort zones and preferred cognitive styles?*

  I'm a planner and a worrier. Much of the strength of my work comes from careful consideration of outcomes, attention to details, and the like. I draw confidence by reducing the potential for surprises, but I also know that wonderful personal learning and useful participant insights come from the unexpected, the serendipitous, the unplanned. So what can I do to place myself in situations where I'm required to call on my own spontaneous resources?

  In other words, how can I develop a creative adaptive openness that taps my unconscious functions, my intuition, insight, and interpretive acuity, and unite these forces with my more ordinary ways of doing business?

- *What is real?*

  This final question is both exciting and troubling. It is increasingly clear that there is no one reality that we all perceive in common. Many unconscious filters of perception exist through which we select, distort, organize, and bring meaning to experience. My experiences in Africa revealed and opened new lenses for me, contributing in a very real sense to who I am.

  Many lenses contribute to our "invention" of reality: the stages of our careers, age, gender, group norms, and a host of considerations from personal history. In fact, the very nature of how our neurology and sense organs function distort reality.

  For example: In an experiment at Harvard Medical School conducted by psychologists Joseph Hubel and David Weisel (Chopra, 1990), one group of kittens were placed in a white box with vertical black stripes. A second group lived in a box with horizontal stripes. A third group was placed in a box that was all white. After being exposed to these conditions during the critical few days when sight develops, the kittens' brains conformed to them for life. For example, the cats raised in the horizontal world were unable to perceive vertically organized objects like furniture legs. This was not because they didn't believe in the existence of vertical stripes, says Chopra, but because their brains did not have the connections to register those perceptions!

This phenomenon is called a *premature cognitive commitment*. Each of us, in an early stage of development, makes certain commitments to "reality." We then mistake the maps we have constructed in our consciousness for the actual territory. We think, in other words, that things are the way they appear to be. This is not true.

Reality, in Chopra's view, depends on who is doing the looking and with what. The eyes of a honeybee cannot perceive the same waves of light that we can. They don't see the usual colors that we do; in fact, they cannot see the flowers but smell the honey from a distance instead. A snake's experience of the same scene would be through infrared radiation. A bat would experience it as an echo of ultrasound.

For a compelling confirmation that things are not the way they appear to be, see the video, *The Color of Fear* (1994). This is a 90-minute film excerpted from a weekend seminar in which several men of different races talk about their experience of racism. It becomes painfully clear to the viewer that American men of African, Hispanic, Chinese, Japanese, and European descent do not occupy the same world even though they would like to and even though they may work side-by-side. One of the white men in this film has a difficult time understanding that "his" America of opportunity and equality is an absolute fiction for a man of color. Double that, by the way, for a woman of color in this country. See *Skin Deep* (Featherston, 1994) for a revealing treatment of the perception of professional women of color in this country. I believe that these two references, *The Color of Fear* and *Skin Deep*, should be required experiences for all educators.

As I engage in self-coaching, then, what actually *is* real? Assuming a less-than-accurate, less-than-complete set of personal perceptions and resulting conclusions, how do I let go of earlier and unconsciously formed cognitive commitments in order to see things in new and nonordinary ways? In other words, how do I keep learning in ways that I cannot predict or guide?

M. Sinetar (1991) counsels that the learning avenues that are open to us for such journeys include *physical adventures* such as walking, canoeing, and martial arts; *reading* and *thinking,* especially outside our fields of expertise; *meditative forms* like journal keeping, solitude, or prayer; *symbols* through enjoyment in theater, nature, music, or fairy tales; *social interactions* with family, friends, and associates; *dreaming;* and *self-observation.*

Paradoxically, it seems that the way to direct my growth most profoundly is to let go of its aim, engaging instead in experiences that invite participation—physically, emotionally, and spiritually, through the fresh eyes of a child.

Indeed, it seems that developing myself personally may be the most productive component of my professional development. Safari, anyone?

Notes from a Safari Journal

In the crater, there is a moment-to-moment existence for resident animals and their human observers. Before 9:00 A.M., two hyenas, rolling unconcernedly in the grass, caught the attention of a wildebeest scout. The herd became alert, and young and old ran for a safer part of the valley floor. Valley, I say, because the Ngorongoro Crater is like no other—ten miles across, rivers and lakes, with elephants, giraffes, rhinos, hippos, gazelles, lions, and more with probably hundreds of birds: flamingos, eagles, marabou storks, ostrich, ibis, kori bustards, and more. Film is expendable here; experiences are not.

What Content Is Most Important?

Juma, our safari guide, seemed to "teach" my wife and me by guiding us through a territory and a world of enlightening experiences. As I reflect on our time with him, it seems he was intuitively working from a hierarchy of learning goals and was committed to engaging us at their most potent level. In Chapter 1, these *nested goals*, were described, each item on the list encompassing the ones before it: activities, engagement, content, dispositions, capacities, and ideals. In this section, I will focus on some special purposes that content can serve in a presentation.

I was still speaking but the audience had gone home! That's a fantasy I entertain occasionally when I'm deciding what content to include in a presentation. Presenters often have far more to say than time allows. How do we decide what is essential to present and what is just nice? In this chapter I will address this question by examining seven purposes of content in a presentation.

Content is meant to include all the information provided by the presenter about the topic. Content, in the context of this chapter, does not include the processes that presenters provide to aid participants in learning the content. (see "Taming the Content-Process Teeter Totter" later in this chapter for a discussion of the dilemma of selecting the proper ratio of content and process.)

Content serves at least seven purposes in a presentation (see Figure 2.4). The reader may wonder if there is an eighth. Actually, I think there is. Perhaps you will identify it before the end of this section.

1. Informs
2. Communicates values
3. Provides theory
4. Establishes credibility
5. Primes the learning pumps
6. Focuses attention
7. Sets a course for action

Figure 2.4: Seven Purposes of Content in a Presentation

Seven Purposes of Content

1. Content informs, so that participants will have increased knowledge of practice, opinions, research, and issues that are useful to them in the deployment of their responsibilities.
2. It communicates values and invites an examination of program and personal congruence with specific values bases.
3. It provides theoretical understanding, so participants can make decisions about why, when, and how to use what they have learned.

4. It establishes credibility for the content or the presenter.
5. It primes the emotional and cognitive pumps to prepare participants for activities.
6. It focuses attention on specific behaviors that are a prerequisite to success in a skills-building exercise.
7. It sets the course for action following a presentation. This can include action to practice and internalize skills after the presentation or action related to communicating with or doing something with others.

Informs

Content for this purpose frequently take the lion's share of presentation time. This seems appropriate, especially in conference settings where people come hungry for information that they can take home to apply in their own situations. This purpose is congruent with the popular mindset that knowledge is something invented by others and given to us. Of course, participants profit from listening to a knowledgeable presenter who distills information and experiences. Content presented to inform can be a valuable catalyst for learning. Content to inform is closely related to two other purposes: the communication of values and the provision of theory.

Communicates Values

When values are clear, decisions are easy. One of the most potent forces for change is the conscious application of personal and organizational values. Too frequently a person's espoused values and acted-upon values are not the same. In a recent study of kindergarten teachers, for example, many teachers reported that each day they violated child growth and development principles in order to meet the requirements of the state curriculum guides. Content that is presented to illuminate values directs the participant's attention to the larger issues. So does content presented to provide theory.

Provides Theory

One could say that this chapter is about theoretical knowledge. Knowledge of theory can help one to understand how something works, why it works the way it does, its relationship to other events and dynamics, and its contributions to the topic being presented. Knowing theory helps participants make decisions; for example, when to use a strategy, when not to use it, and possible alternative approaches when a specific strategy is not appropriate. Theory then becomes a foundation for developing practices that utilize, in unique form, core principles. The "theoretical" information presented in this chapter is intended to affect presenters' decisions about what content to include in a presentation plan and what to eliminate during the presentation if there is more content than time permits.

Establishes Credibility

Speaker credibility and audience confidence in the sources of the speaker's material are important because without this, audiences may be polite, but they will not be receptive enough to seriously consider the message. Credibility can usually be established with just a few comments. A workshop participant told me recently that she found me credible precisely because I did *not* introduce myself with an exhaustive review of titles, publications and experience, but because I spoke with confidence and moved directly to the heart of the topic. Speaker credibility can be established at the opening of a session by succinctly citing relevant figures or other data and by communicating a sense of being well read, current, and knowledgeable. Skillful speakers establish source credibility by referencing studies, commissions, or authors in relation to major themes in the presentation.

Primes Pumps, and Focuses Attention

Sometimes I tell participants a story about being on a zip line. I detail the experience of being terrified, looking down from the mountaintop to the valley below. I describe gripping the handles on the pulley mechanism that rides the cable over my head, perspiring, afraid that my hands will slip, causing me to fall, and how, at the moment I step from the platform and begin the descent, I pass from terror into ecstasy. Such a story primes the emotional pump for a group about to engage in a learning exercise involving some risk. That is, it encourages participants to locate within themselves the emotional resources that are necessary to risk and to learn. Similarly, cognitive pump priming helps participants bring information from long-term storage into working memory. Presenters may do this, for example, by reminding participants of the attributes of a well-performed skill just before they engage in a practice session.

Pump priming and attention focusing represent two good reasons to invest workshop time on content because they help participants produce maximum learning from the skills-building processes that follow. To teach meeting facilitation, for example, I will demonstrate facilitation strategies before group members practice. During the demonstration some participants are instructed to pay attention to what I say, others to notice the facilitation techniques being used, and still others to observe nonverbal communication. Focusing detailed attention on important dimensions in a demonstration consistently contributes to practice results of high quality.

Sets a Course for Action

Speakers may foreshadow two types of action for audiences. In one case, presenters prepare participants to practice and refine skills, or apply what has been learned. The second type of action is a call to communicate, influence others, vote, or engage in some other political activity. In each case, this is a valuable use of presentation time, for influencing what participants do after the presentation is usually the ultimate aim of the session.

It may be good strategy to deliver this type of content before nearing the end of a presentation. A time crunch usually becomes apparent near the end of a session and a presenter may rush through the final content without communicating the full importance of an action plan. In addition, if people have to leave early, they will miss the action message.

Skillful presenters include four elements in a call to action. They discuss a *rationale*, elaborating on why the action is important to the learner or the organization. They offer specific ideas or *structures* for how to proceed. They set *expectations* for frequency and timing. (For example, "Please complete two coaching cycles before returning here at the end of the month.") Finally, they foreshadow possible *resistances*, procrastinations, and awkwardness that learners may experience, and contextualize these as part of the normal learning process, something to be experienced with foreknowledge and perseverance.

The Content versus Time Dilemma

I have two hours of content and forty-five minutes of time—what do I leave out? Three questions guide experienced presenters in resolving this persistent design dilemma. First, they remind themselves of the overall goal of the presentation, often stated in terms of what knowledge, skills, attitudes, or action is envisioned for participants. Second, they ask themselves what relevance this goal has to the longer-term goals that are related to the dispositions, capacities, or ideals described in the Chapter 1 section, "When the Presenter Is a Guide." Third, they examine the intended contribution of each content segment in relation to the seven purposes described above. Fourth, and finally, they ask themselves how essential each piece of content is to achieving the immediate and long term outcomes for this session.

In other words, during both the design and the presentation phase, the following self-talk is useful to presenters: "What's my purpose? Am I including this content because I love talking about it, or is it really essential?"

Postscript

Is there an eighth purpose for content? I think so. Content can also entertain, relax, and increase audience receptivity to the other seven purposes in the presentation. Laughter is a particularly valuable resource toward these ends. It affects many positive physiological functions, including causing "a drop in the pulse rate, the secretion of endorphins, and increased oxygen in the blood. It has been found to liberate creativity and provoke such higher-level thinking skills as anticipation, finding novel relationships, and visual imagery" (Costa, 1991). In Chapter 5 I discuss presentation humor. When the audience is laughing, they won't leave the presentation before you do.

Taming the Content-Process Teeter-Totter

To "fail forward" is to learn from experiences that produce different results from those intended. Several years ago I delivered the worst presentation I had ever done, before or since. Not only did the audience know it was bad, but *I* knew it was bad, yet I couldn't stop myself from the behaviors that were creating agony for all of us. Such is the power of the untamed content-process teeter-totter.

I persisted because of good intentions, overzealousness, and the misguided notion that delivering content is the sole purpose of presentations. I had been scheduled for a three-hour Friday night presentation and a full day on Saturday. The topic was "meeting facilitation." A heavy rainstorm delayed my flight arrival time; thus I missed the Friday evening session entirely. I resolved to "make up" the content that participants had lost by collapsing the one-and-a-half-day presentation into Saturday. The distressed faces of those trapped participants are still burned into my memory, making the experience so painful that I learned an irreversible lesson about the content-process teeter-totter: *My content is not as important as the audience's interaction with the content!*

Michael Doyle and David Strauss (1993) use the metaphor of gum chewing to describe the dilemma that meeting facilitators face with content and process. The issue for presenters is similar. Consider "gum" to be the content you bring to your audience. Consider "chewing" to be the interactive process you provide to assist participants in receiving, processing, and applying the content. How much gum and how much chewing you provide becomes a dominant question in presentation design.

What I learned on that painful rainy day is that the content I bring to a presentation has little or no value unless audience members chew it in some form. This simple realization has removed the burden of feeling that I must always follow my plan, report all my research, or use all my notes.

But how does one know the appropriate ratio of content and process to provide? Decisions about this are made at two stages of the presentation. First, in the design stage, the types of presentation goals are determined and decisions are made about the size of the conceptual units to present. Second, during the actual presentation, judgments are made about degrees of learning accomplishment, unanticipated needs of the learners, rapport, and participant resourcefulness. These "show time" perceptions often override the decisions that were made during the planning stage.

Although content-process ratios can't be described in percentages, a logical progression of increased processing time exists as one's goals move from the acquisition of knowledge to the development of attitudes, skills, and commitment to apply what has been learned. To illustrate: In a World War II experiment that was considered a breakthrough in the social sciences, Kurt Lewin tried to get Iowa housewives to purchase the less popular but highly nutritious cuts of meat, such as liver, heart, kidney, and sweetbreads. Lectures were given to three groups about the desirability of buying the organ meats. No group discussion was provided. Three other groups received the same information and, in addition, were given an opportunity to discuss the data among themselves. In follow-ups, it was discovered that the lecture plus discussion method was ten times as effective at changing behavior. The first groups achieved a 3 percent behavior change, the second, 32 percent (Eitington, 1984). Figure 2.5 represents this theoretical need for a progression from less to more processing time, depending on the type of goal, and suggests intervals for processing activities. Please keep in mind that these are generalizations *only,* and that many good reasons can exist for deviating from these patterns.

The purposes and types of processes will also vary according to the presenter's goal. To develop awareness and knowledge, presentations are often information intensive. Listeners must be given opportunities to mentally organize the data, check their understandings, and compare the data to personal experiences. Without this, highly dense information presentations will put participants in positions of sustained passive listening, but not learning, because the learner's manipulation of information is essential to creating personal relevance and retention.

For attitude outcomes, the primary purpose of processes may be to help participants make meaning of an experience. Figure 2.5 shows processing occurring before content delivery to illustrate just one of many designs that will stimulate attitude change. In this design an experience (a process) is followed by an analysis (more process) of the experience. In another design, David Johnson and Roger Johnson (1994) describe an instructional procedure called "structured academic controversies." In this five-step process, pairs of learners (1)

TYPES OF PRESENTATION GOALS	CONTENT ------ PROCESS XXXX
Awareness	--------X-----------X----------X---------X-----
Knowledge Acquisition	--------X-----------X----------X---------X-----
Skills Acquisition	------------XXXX-----XXXX-----XXXX---------
Attitude Development	XXXXXXXXXXXXXX---------------------------
Application	-----------X------------X--------------XXXXXXX

Figure 2.5: Content-Process Ratios and Timing

develop a position and decide how to present it to others, (2) present their position, then listen to and take notes of a presentation of the opposing position, (3) meet with the opposing pairs to discuss the two positions, criticize ideas (not people), and assess the degree of evidence and logic supporting each position, (4) reverse positions with the opposing pairs and present each others' views, and (5) drop all advocacy and work with the opposing pairs to present the best evidence and reasoning from both sides. The Johnsons report that these procedures produce high achievement and retention, transfer of learning to new situations, and generalization of principles.

Marilyn Tabor and I recently used a variation on this theme with several school site councils in a workshop on "Living Effectively with Conflict." (By the way, I like that title better than "managing" conflict because it presumes that conflict is a natural consequence of living and that the human animal, like the wildlife in the Serengeti, can learn to work with it.) We introduced the topic in a twenty-minute period of total silence in which each member (1) privately brainstormed one's own assumptions about conflict, (2) selected the one assumption that had the greatest influence in affecting choices in one's work setting, (3) wrote that one assumption on a sentence strip and—still silently—posted it on an easel, and (4) silently read the sentence strips as they were posted and recorded one's intellectual and emotional reactions to other group members' posted assumptions in a journal. We then offered tips on safe ways of dialoguing about these assumptions. Before we offered any "content" of our own on this topic, most of the deep learning had already been done.

An important design decision that presenters make is how to organize concepts and information into presentation units. Because the limit of working memory is about seven items of information, in highly technical presentations no more than five important facts should be presented before participants have a chance to process the data. For less fact-intensive content, processing time might be planned to occur at regular fifteen-to-twenty-minute intervals.

When decision making about content-process ratios occurs during the presentation itself, presenters need to be able to make decisions on their feet, even when they countermand the decisions made in the planning stage. I was recently reminded of this as I began the afternoon of a full-day session. The public agenda said "Coaching Competencies." Since the agenda was so artfully vague, I could eliminate portions of my planned (but not communicated) content without the participants feeling that they were missing out on anything. This allowed me time to address their need to interact and relate the content to their own experiences. In this case more process time than I had planned was crucial for participants to be able to accept a new perspective. My broadly painted public agenda and my reading of participants allowed me to drop content, meet the unanticipated needs of the group, and not repeat my earlier painful experience.

Of course, there are many other on-their-feet-decision opportunities that presenters encounter. One of these is the after-lunch sleepiness syndrome. I explore this in the "Awake and Learning after Lunch" section of Chapter 3.

Using Organizers to Save Preparation Time

A few years before my wanderings in equatorial Africa, I took an assignment much farther north. It was a long weekend and a delightfully sunny one for Denmark for that time of year. Because of this, people had left Copenhagen for the countryside, and my wife and I were unprepared for the convoys of holidayers trying to ride the ferry from Odense back to Copenhagen on a Sunday afternoon. A friendly Dane in a Saab ahead of us explained what was happening and advised us that we would have about a three-hour wait before we would be able to board. This being the case, I turned to the notes in my briefcase, and with Sue's help, began to plan the two-hour presentation that I had been asked to make to members of the World Health Organization (WHO) the next day.

Not too long ago, I might have agonized about the structure of that presentation for more time than it took to deliver it. This is often a problem for presenters, because they want to get the best possible results from a presentation but have limited time in which to prepare. As I've learned from painful experience, devoting energy to struggling with structure is not the best use of planning time. Deciding more important issues, like presentation goals, content, and delivery, is a better investment of time because these get to the heart of the learning experience—its essence and achievement, not the mechanics of organizing it.

Recently Bruce Wellman and I explored issues related to presentation planning and discovered the notion of organizers—formal structures, frameworks, "baskets," or "containers" into which the presenter can "drop" his or her content (Garmston and Wellman, 1992). Using presentation organizers saves planning time. To use them, a presenter must know four things:

- the type of presentation goal and the allocated time
- information about the audience
- a variety of presentation organizers, from which the presenter can pick the best fit for the other two considerations

Type of Goal and Allocated Time

We speak to inform, to request action, to motivate, to entertain, and to instruct. Consider these settings.

Scenario 1: A fifteen-minute presentation to a parents club to request volunteers for a project. You have printed materials.

Scenario 2: A forty-minute keynote to a large group in an auditorium setting. You have no printed materials.

Scenario 3: A ninety-minute presentation to develop awareness-level knowledge for a group of veteran teachers. You have handouts.

Scenario 4: A thirty-minute board report requesting project approval for an innovative program serving handicapped students. You have printed materials.

Scenario 5: A ten-minute presentation to an administrative team, requesting its participation in a moderately high-risk leadership staff development project. You have no printed materials.

In each case, materials, the constraints of time, and the presenter's goal—what he or she wants participants to do as a result of the presentation—interacts to affect the type of presentation container that will be most useful. My purpose in Denmark was to motivate and instruct.

Information about the Audience

Two types of audience information are useful in selecting containers. First, what is generally known about the audience? Is it a decision-making group, and if so, what formats are typically presented to it? How will furniture be arranged and what limitations might that create? What are the norms for this group for interaction in presentations? Some high school faculties, for example, sometimes expect more lecture and less processing time than elementary school groups.

The second type of information concerns the immediate emotional environment. Is this a mandatory meeting? Is there anything in the recent history of this group that might affect its receptivity to you, the topic, or *any* presentation made to them at this time? For example, I was once asked to speak to a group that had recently received a memo explaining that in this first year of a new employee performance review system, far too many "excellents" were awarded. The situation was to be corrected next year by increased training of supervisors. Can you imagine this group's state of mind regarding any presentation, particularly a mandatory one (which this one was)?

What did I know about the group I was to work with in Denmark? It was an ad hoc group of WHO professionals. They would attend the session voluntarily, out of desire to increase the effectiveness of presentations they made; they each spoke several languages; they gave presentations in formal and informal settings, to large and small groups, to government officials and to professionals and citizens interested in the field of health.

Presentation Containers

Research shows that listeners remember better and remember more if they know the organization of the talk. The best presenters, then, are not only deliberate in choosing the organizing features of their presentation but also make these boldly obvious to the audience. Containers may sometimes be the entire organization for a presentation. (For example, the first two containers listed below can be used for an entirely unrehearsed speech.) At other times a presentation may employ several containers within the context of a formal opening and closing. Here are four time-tested and effective containers.

- **Two Questions**

  This container is useful for both extemporaneous presentations and planned ones. The presenter says, "Two questions are most frequently asked about this topic. They are ____ and ____. Let me speak about each of them."

  The speaker then uses this as a framework for the balance of the talk. What is the origin of the questions? Often they are merely an invention of the presenter, to be used as a device around which to organize information.

- **Three Ideas**

  This container can be used in impromptu settings as well as planned ones. The presenter decides what information is most important to deliver and organizes it around three main ideas. For example, if you were designing a brief session on the topic of developing leadership credibility, you might say:

  > There are three components to a credibility-building model: (1) clarity—clarification of the leader's and the constituent's needs, interest, values, visions, aims, and aspirations, (2) unity—people must be united in a common cause, and (3) intensity—this exists when core values are the basis for operating principles, decisions, and resource allocation. (Kouzes and Posner, 1993). My comments today will address each of these in turn.

- **Compare-Contrast**

  When you're presenting a choice between two or more alternatives (people, programs, equipment), an excellent organizer is the compare-contrast container. This approach gives your audience a detailed, side-by-side comparison of each alternative. To compare teacher evaluation with Cognitive

Coaching,sm for example, you would list key attributes: who sets the observation and conference focus, who makes judgments about what is good or bad, what is done with the data. Then you would speak about each attribute and how it is treated in the two systems.

One tip about the compare-contrast framework: It allows you to add punch to your ideas by using spatial anchoring—standing in one spot to describe evaluation and a different spot to describe coaching. When your verbal and nonverbal communications are congruent, audience members' understandings are enhanced. A natural strategy to support learners in organizing and integrating the information is to have small groups develop Venn diagrams, showing what is the same and different in the two positions.

- **Problem-Solution**

  This is one of the most exciting containers for me, because of its versatility and logical appeal. Developed by Communication Associates, it is a nine-step organizer delivered in this sequence.

1. *Anecdote*. Tell a brief story in which a problem is illustrated that relates to your topic.
2. *Problem*. State the problem that the anecdote illustrates.
3. *Importance*. Say why this is an important issue.
4. *Credibility*. Here you establish your own credibility. What gives you the authority to speak on this topic? Perhaps it is reading you have been doing, personal experiences, or people you have consulted.
5. *Solution*. Name or state the solution. For example, as you may be beginning to notice, I've used the problem-solution container as an organizer for this chapter and have named the solution to the problem of best use of preparation time as "containers."
6. *Subpoints*. List about three supporting ideas for the solution. In this chapter they are: (1) type of goal and allocated time, (2) information about the audience, and (3) information about containers. Completing these first six steps provides the frame for the body of the presentation, which you will make in the next step.
7. *Essential details*. Now elaborate on each of the subpoints. This becomes the body of the presentation.
8. *Future*. Provide examples of how this solution will benefit the audience. For example, in this chapter I

stress that one of the major benefits of containers, as long as you have routinized a few, is that they save preparation time, freeing you from planning to focus on other important issues related to the presentation.

9. *Action*. This is the close of your presentation. Now you ask for approval—a vote, a signature, an allocation of funds, or a commitment to try the ideas you have presented.

So, to save time in the preparation of your next presentation, I'd invite you to invest a little upfront time taking an inventory of the presentation containers you know. You may wish to check or augment your list with the four examples listed here and the several more that can be found in the Garmston and Wellman book cited earlier (1992). When you do that, I think you'll find the increase in time saving and confidence well worth the effort.

Designing for Collaboration

Recently a colleague returned to classroom teaching after three years on a special staff development project. She was excited about being able to apply what she had learned from those three years to the classroom. Yet she was soon inundated with the "daily demands of the production line" and a terrible sense of isolation. After months of collaborating with others about the design and delivery of presentations to adults, she was shocked at the absence of those opportunities in her new school and, even more, shocked that the teachers with whom she was working had no real idea of how isolated they were. In other words, they took for granted that the aloneness with which they worked was normal.

This story illustrates how pervasive separateness, disconnectedness, and isolation is for educators. Many teachers perceive this as an appropriate way to conduct business; it is not. A faculty's capacity to achieve rich student learning lies in a sense of community, not isolation. It lies in collaboration skills, learning from one another, and valuing interdependence. As staff development matures, there is a growing recognition of the influence that the culture of the workplace has on teachers' cognition, attitudes, and behavior, and of the positive influence that staff development can have on work culture.

Emerging presentation practices seek ways to create communities of dialogue among educators in order to solve problems, learn more about teaching and learning, and increase organizational effectiveness for student learning. They promote opportunities for professional reflection, inquiry, and collaboration and attempt to correct three main dysfunctions in our institutions: fragmentation, competition, and reactiveness. These are not merely problems to be solved, "they are frozen patterns of thought to be dissolved" (Kofman and Senge, 1993).

In this section I explore three practical ideas that presenters can use to exceed expectations by serving a second agenda—increasing the capacities for collaboration—regardless of the presentation topic. A foundation for this can be found in: Garmston (1991), Garmston and Wellman (1992), and Costa and Garmston (1994). These three ideas for dual-agenda presentations are: (1) precede group learning activities with a rationale for developing collaboration, (2) engage active group learning, and (3) focus reflection on the development of sociocentric thinking.

Provide a Rationale

Ask participants to exchange seats with someone sitting in a different part of the room, without explaining why. Some resistance will be natural.

As an alternative approach, explain in advance that when one sits in the same seat all the time, one tends to see the same things, and says the same things. However, when changing one's seat, one changes one's perspective and one's neighbors. Sameness is exchanged for newness, and energy and ideas are stimulated. After explaining this, ask them to exchange seats.

As the presenter, you will realize two benefits. Responsiveness replaces resistance and the group understands that interdependence is an overarching goal in this presentation. An understood goal guides learners' consciousness and behavior. Since adults' willingness to engage in activities increases when those activities make sense, a brief commercial of rationale is worth its weight in presentation gold.

So too is the public valuing of interdependence and conscious modeling of constructivist learning. Since both of these ideals are also appropriate for students, the following set of constructivist principles may have special meaning for staff developers.

Engage Active Group Learning

If staff development were a political campaign, we might print buttons that say, "It's the *construction* of learning, stupid!"—reminding ourselves that adults, too, construct learning from processing experiences. Consider the principles of constructivism shown in Figure 2.6 as you design your next presentation or workshop.

1. Learning is an active, not a passive, process.
2. Learning is enhanced by sociocentric, not egocentric, thinking. Rich learning occurs when learners share ideas, inquire, and solve problems together.
3. Learning beyond rote occurs when learners have opportunities to make sense of new knowledge and to create meaning for themselves based upon individual and shared experiences.
4. Reflection and metacognition contribute to the construction of knowledge. Public discussion and thinking out loud increase an individual learner's capacity and add to the collective knowledge of the group.
5. New learning is mediated by prior experience, values, and beliefs.

Figure 2.6: Five Potent Principles of Learning

Bruce Wellman and Laura Lipton (1991) offer a model for constructivist teaching that they use with adults as well as students. Their teaching-learning cycle defines three phases of instruction: (1) activating and engaging prior knowledge, (2) exploring and discovering, and (3) organizing and integrating old and new information. Each phase is accomplished within a learning environment of purposeful group tasks, ongoing authentic assessment, and specific cognitive goals for each phase. Here are some examples.

- **Activating and Engaging Prior Knowledge**
  You are making a presentation on the topic of presenting to adults. You open with this small group activity. "Compare presenting to adults and teaching students. What is similar? What is different? What conclusions do you draw regarding your work in this area?" Or, you ask groups to list what they know, think they know, and want to know, about the topic.
- **Exploring and Discovering**
  You invite trios to observe a skillfully performed Cognitive Coaching[sm] transaction. At its conclusion you ask them to analyze the coach's use of language, interview the person being coached for his or her response to the coach's questions, and interview the coach to learn what principles and data were guiding the coach's decisions. Or, in another example,

you elicit a partner's hypotheses about a topic and ask to read a document, seeking validation or reversals.

- **Organizing and Integrating**
  You have small groups make graphic organizers that display the relationships of the concepts that have been learned. Or, you ask the group to develop performance criteria at the expert, developing, and novice levels of a task, then present and self-assess performance.

Focus Reflection on the Development of Sociocentric Thinking

It has been said that adults do not learn from experience, they learn from the *processing* of experience. For this reason, when presenting with a dual agenda, it is essential to focus individual and group reflection on ways in which group learning activities contribute to participants' knowledge of one another and insights about working effectively as members of a learning community. Private reflection and writing in journals, followed by group discussion, will build collective knowledge about and valuing of adult collaboration. Here are some reflections I've been testing after a group has finished a learning task together.

> Take a moment and reflect on the decisions you made about your participation as a group member in this task. What did you decide? How did that guide your behavior? What results did that produce for you and the group?
>
> What are you observing about yourselves as a community of learners? What inferences do you draw from those observations?
>
> List anything you thought during this group activity but did not say. What influence did that have on your participation in the activity? How might you have said what you were thinking in a manner that would be respectful and supportive of the group?

As you use this dual-agenda approach to presenting—always promoting interdependence—you give far more than you were asked because you help the group develop its capacity for learning together, creating together, and making school more effective for students and enjoyable for adults. I think you'll also be pleased to observe groups develop over time, as they require fewer collaborative commercials from you and take over with increasing depth and complexity the design of their own learning activities and reflective processes.

Endnotes

Chopra, D. (1990). *Quantum Healing: Exploring the Frontiers of Mind/Body Medicine*. New York: Bantam Books.

Costa, A. (1991). The search for intelligent life. In A. Costa (ed.). *Developing Minds: A Resource Book for Teaching Thinking*, Vol. 1. Alexandria, VA: Association for Supervision and Curriculum Development.

Costa, A. & Garmston, R. (1994). *Cognitive Coaching: A Foundation for Renaissance Schools*. Norwood, MA: Christopher-Gordon Publishers, Inc.

Covey, S. (1989). *The Seven Habits of Highly Effective People*. New York: Simon & Schuster.

Doyle, M. & Strauss, D. (1993) *How to Make Meetings Work: The New Interaction Method*. New York: Berkeley Publishing Group.

Eitington, J. (1984). *The Winning Trainer*. Houston, TX: Gulf Publishing Co.

Featherston, Elena (editor). (1994). *Skin Deep:* Women Writing on Color, Culture and Identity. Freedom, CA: The Crossing Press.

Fullan, M. (1993). *Change Forces: Probing the Depths of Educational Reform*. Bristol, PA: Falmer Press.

Garmston, R. (1991). Staff developers as social architects. *Educational Leadership* 49(3): 64–65.

Garmston, R. & Wellman, B. (1992). *How to Make Presentations That Teach and Transform*. Alexandria, VA: Association for Supervision and Curriculum Development.

Johnson, D. & Johnson, R. (1994). Constructive conflict in the schools. *Journal of Social Issues* 50(1): 117–137.

Kofman, F. & Senge, P. (1993). Communities of commitment: The heart of learning organizations. *Organizational Dynamics* (Autumn): pp. 5–23.

Kouzes, J.M. & Posner, B.Z. (1993). *Credibility: How Leaders Gain and Lose It, Why People Demand It*. San Francisco: Jossey-Bass.

McPhee, D. (1992). Music: Easy and fast way to accelerate learning. *AL&T Network Newsletter* 1(1): 1–2.

Sinetar, M. (1991). *Developing a 21st Century Mind*. New York: Villard Books.

Smith, R. (1984). *Making Successful Presentations: A Self-Teaching Guide*. New York: John Wiley & Sons, Inc.

Wah, Lee Mun (Director). (1994). *The Color of Fear*. Berkeley, CA: Stir Fry Productions, (510)419-3930.

Wellman, B. & Lipton, L. Making meaning: Linking primary science and literature. Presented at the 1991 Association for Supervision and Curriculum Development National Conference, San Francisco.

SAFARI SUPPLIES
WE DELIVER!
PIZZA

CHAPTER 3

How to Deliver Effective Presentations

We can, whenever and wherever we choose, successfully teach all children whose schooling is of interest to us. We already know more than we need to do that. Whether or not we do it must finally depend on how we feel about the fact that we haven't so far.

—Ron Edmonds, Metropolitan Detroit Association of Black School Educators Newsletter

Effective delivery demands vision, sound maps, perseverance, and a willingness to keep learning. For the presenter who serves as a guide in the treasured territory of developing learning cultures, to keep learning is a passion. Good delivery also requires a repertoire of moves while in the field. This chapter explores effective openings, audience rapport, podium humor, speaking to parent groups, maintaining momentum, keeping audiences energized, giving "value added" presentations, teaching for transfer, using learning instruments, answering audience questions, nonverbal communications, and closings. The tips about these topics represent the collective wisdom of many acclaimed presenters and show the way to similar levels of achievement.

Openings

It was the first day of the work year for thirty administrators. They were gathered in the board room of their district office for a two-day seminar. Jeff Peltier, staff development director for the nearby North Thurston School District in Lacey, Washington, and I had planned an opening that involved (1) a welcome, (2) a role survey, (3) some cartoon transparencies, (4) a description of workshop goals and an agenda, and (5) a small-group discussion of what was pleasing them and troubling them about supervising teachers. As Jeff and I listened to people and observed the preopening energy in the room, we were clear that our planned opening had a good chance of producing counterproductive results. We had energy in the room. That was good, but it was ricocheting off the walls and the people in ways that defied our attempts to focus the group.

One problem presenters frequently face is how to *focus, energize,* and *establish rapport* with the audience in the first three to five minutes. This is a critical period because norms are established in the first moments of the relationship. Momentum developed at the outset in these three areas can save time and create learning gains later. From observing other presenters, conducting hundreds of my own presentations, consulting with experts, and reading the literature, I'm collecting a range of strategies to achieve these three opening states. Here are a few.

Focus

We anticipated that the problem with the administrator group described above was going to be focus, and possibly rapport. Lack of energy would not be a problem. In fact, there was abundant energy, but none of it was headed in the direction that Jeff and I wanted. Prior to our opening, the group was animated and so engaged in informal discussion of the district agendas that Jeff and I actually felt excluded from opening conversations among participants. Our challenge was to ride the high energy in the room and redirect it to our topic.

Normally, focus can be achieved through a variety of rather straightforward strategies. Describing the goals and agenda, eliciting participant concerns about the topic, delivering a startling statement or statistic related to the topic, or posing a problem question are some examples. But in this situation, we first had to get the group's attention.

We did this by inserting a trios metaphor discussion before step five (a supervisor is like a jackknife because...), light enough to parallel the high and humorous energy in the room yet serious enough to direct the energy toward our topic.

Here are some opening moves that will focus a group.

- **State the Purpose of the Presentation**

  Today's purpose is to extend the capacities of teams to work effectively together.

  My purpose today is to support you in the work you are doing in getting your expertise used by others.

Brief, clear statements let participants know why they are there and how the topic relates to them. Notice that both comments are statements of *sufficiency* which presume that knowledge and resources already exist on the topic, rather than *deficiency* (I am here to fix your abysmal ignorance), which produces distance between the presenter and the audience. Notice, too, that each is artfully vague. Such statements are best made within the first minute or two of your comments. Later, if appropriate, specific learning goals for the session can be identified.

- **Preview the Agenda**
  With a posted public agenda, preferably on chart paper so that it can be used throughout the presentation to mark where you are, offer some explanatory comments as follows:

  We will open this topic with an inventory in which you can assess the current practices of collaboration used by your team. Following that, we will explore some troubling research findings related to the impact of collaboration on staff efficacy and student learning. Next we will relate that to a set of recommendations for you to consider.

  Your comments help group members make sense of the visual agenda, serve as an advanced organizer for their learning, foreshadow key points you wish to make, or underscore the relative importance of sections ("you may find this section of the presentation the most important for you to take home and use immediately").

On the public agenda is: (1) welcome, (2) overview, (3) inventory, (4) research, and (5) recommendations.

- **Make A Startling Statement**

  I do not have much time with you today. In fact I only have time enough to annoy you. And I plan to do this, much like a grain of sand annoys an oyster.

I once heard a presenter open with that statement. She had my attention for sure!

Statistics and facts can also grab an audience's attention when they relate your topic. Consider the following facts on the indicated topics.

Forecasting: The telephone was considered to be an impractical toy, according to early Western Union officials.

Regional differences: Yellow lights in Washington, D.C. last longer than those in New York City. Traffic-flow engineers take many factors into account when setting the timing of traffic lights.

Among these are assumptions that the reaction time of the average driver is one second; the minimum time to accomplish major movement in an intersection is fifteen seconds; and, the higher the approach speed, the longer the yellow light needs to be. If you are in Washington, this fact is of interest; in Tampa, ho hum.

The hidden nature of cumulative effects: A typical credit card charges 18 percent interest. How long will it take to pay off a $1,750 balance, meeting the 2 percent minimum payment required each month? It will take nearly twenty-two years, and you will pay $4,000 in interest!

What schools should teach: One hundred entry-level custodial, janitorial, and laborer jobs opened up in Los Angeles during one brief period in 1996. Twenty-five hundred people applied. The work ethic in America is alive and well. The market for low-skilled and semi-skilled jobs is not.

American schools or educators: America has a teaching corps of 2.8 million persons.

Adaptivity: McDonalds opened its first restaurant in India in 1996. But where is the beef? This New Delhi restaurant serves mutton burgers and vegetable nuggets.

- **Pose A Problem**
  Another move that can rivet a group's mental energy is to describe a perplexing and persistent problem, then add that the purpose of today's work will be to address that issue.

  Remember your last walk by the primary grades. Recall where the kindergarten classes are placed. Can you see some of these kids in your mind's eye? Ten of them will not make it through your school system. Which ones? What can you do about it today?

Energize

While this group of administrators was displaying abundant but topic-unrelated energy, the *absence* of energy is more common and may be more difficult to address. Why are some groups "energyless"? It depends. Participants report a range of reasons for opening blues and nonparticipation. These include not *wanting* to be there, social discomfort from not knowing other participants or feeling like they are low in the role hierarchy represented, limited understanding of topic relevance, not knowing *why* they are there, anxiety about "performing" well in the workshop, organizational stress (e.g., recent distribution of reduction-in-force notices within the district), or just plain fatigue. Since mental and emotional energy can be directed either internally (my thoughts, feelings, concerns, sensations, attitudes) or externally (the environment, the topic, other participants, what's going to happen), and a presentation requires commonly focused external energy, the presenter's job is to get the energy externalized and flowing in roughly the same direction.

Since physiological changes ensure changes in energy and emotional state, one road to energizing is to get people moving. Have participants sit with someone they don't know, do a birthday line-up, stand up and interview several other participants, or rearrange the furniture. Another approach is to direct their collective attention to some topic-related activity. In pairs, have them list and share their personal goals for the workshop, or have them list what they know, want to know, or think they know about the topic. Or, in small groups, have them list their concerns or develop causal theories for a current situation (e.g., many of our most intellectually capable teachers are leaving the profession) and give possible solutions.

I've found that such opening idea-generating exercises with pairs, trios, or quartets not only energize, they also illuminate the purpose for being there and help me establish rapport with the group. In addition, they are sound instructional practices because they support learners in activating their prior knowledge, their thinking about their knowledge, and their engagement with other learners.

Establish Rapport

During the first few minutes of a presentation, most audience members are hard at work making judgments about the presenter's credibility, the topic's relevance to their interests, and the personal benefits-loss ratio of attending the session. As described in the section "Before the Opening" in Chapter 2, it's useful for the presenter to stand still at the opening to aid participants in making judgments—but not for too long. Many presenters make it a rule to engage the audience within the first five minutes in the types of idea-generating small-group discussions mentioned above. This shifts attention from the speaker and redirects it where it most properly belongs, to the relationship with the audience and the collective expertise in the group.

Since rapport is the product of credibility, respect, and perceived personal concern and similarities, a range of beginning activities can hasten this connection between the presenter and the participants: preopening one-on-one conversations (I care about and am interested in you); presentation of an agenda (I'm organized, know where I'm going, and respect your time); invitations to proactively attend to comfort and learning needs

(I know you're adults with unique styles and interests, and I respect that); use of names and eye contact (this is a personal communication between us); humor (let's not take this or me too seriously, we have permission to have fun); and clear and visible motives (I am personal with you when I share, without pretense, my intentions in this relationship, and you don't have to worry about hidden agendas).

Focus, energy, and rapport. Is one of these significantly more important than the others in a presentation opening? Yes and no! No, because all three are inextricably intertwined in their support of quickly producing an optimum learning environment for adults. For example, when Jeff and I were able to focus the administrator group described earlier, we also drew ourselves into their inner circle of energy, and we developed focus and rapport. Yes, because relationship is the ultimate context and foundation for learning. In fact, rapport most often generates responsiveness, as it did with our administrator group.

Notes from a Safari Journal

I'm very pleased that Juma is our guide. Sue is, too. We both like him and can't imagine what it would be like to be in such close quarters for so long with a guide with whom we felt tense.

Audience Rapport

I vividly remember losing rapport with a group of high school teachers in a summer workshop. Some were with me, but an appreciable number had dropped out. There were side conversations, that agonizing-to-look-at lifeless slump, single elbows propping up dejected heads. It was swelteringly hot, and instead of air conditioning, an array of electric fans caused hearing problems as they sluggishly moved the warm, moist air about the room.

I reviewed my options. While focus, energy, and rapport are top priorities during openings, I regard *audience rapport* as being one of three persistent presenter goals throughout the presentation. The other two are *developing audience resourcefulness* and *accelerating adult learning* (Berry and Garmston, 1987). Rapport is first because without it, a presenter and an audience achieve nothing.

One meaning of rapport is, literally, that people are responsive to you. That's the desired condition in working with an audience, and clearly, for some of these teachers, I had lost it.

My instinctive reaction in such settings is to do *anything* different, so I began, in this four-hour presentation, to (1) vary the pace, (2) schedule breaks, (3) increase the number of activities, and (4) arrange and announce a change into a cooler room for the next day's session. We adjourned, but we still lacked full rapport.

That evening, I reviewed what I know about establishing rapport (see Figure 3.1).

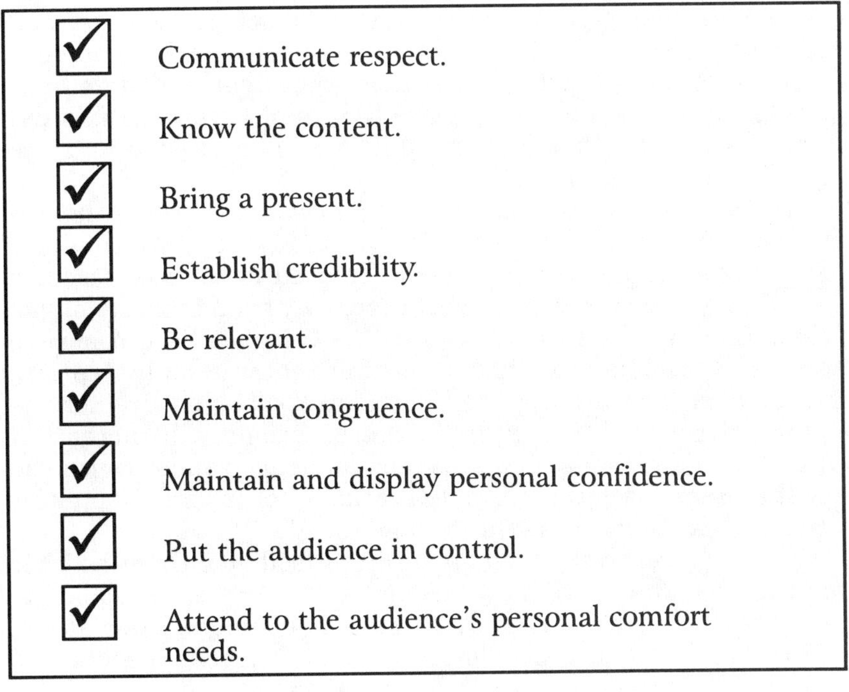

Figure 3.1: Establishing Rapport

I rated myself okay on all but communicating respect, being relevant, and putting the audience in control. Because of that, maintaining and displaying personal confidence was also beginning to slip.

There are many ways that presenters communicate respect: starting on time, being prepared and organized, acknowledging group expertise, and previewing and negotiating an agenda. It was on this last point that I might do some work. While the scheduled topic was peer coaching, only about one-third were currently coaching; one-third were neutral—that is, they might or might not decide to peer coach as a result of this presentation; and, I think, one-third were distressed or fearful about the topic. For some, the topic just wasn't a useful "gift."

I resolved to do three things. First, I would put the audience in charge by scheduling a negotiation of the remainder of our time together, eliciting from those least involved a topic of interest to them that I could address and that related to the larger topic (collegiality), of which peer coaching is just a part.

This move of putting the audience in control of content effectively breaks the typical child-adult relationship into which even sophisticated groups can slip. As teachers know, children may adopt roles of accepting no responsibility for their learning. They then behave dependently on the adult. "Teach me, amuse me," they seem to say when they take this position. Getting audience input on content priorities, time allocations, learning-style preferences, and personal concerns are ways of reversing this dynamic in the relationship and putting the audience and the presenter on an equal footing.

The second and related move I made was to increase the relevance of what I had already planned to present by frequently providing examples of how it could be used in their classrooms even if they never decided to peer coach. My friend and colleague Laura Lipton calls these "you gets." A "you get" is a concrete, specific example of an application that requires no interpretation or transfer thinking from participants. Generally, increasing the density of "you gets" in presentations will increase a practitioner's satisfaction as well as audience rapport with the speaker. See "Teaching on Triple Tracks" later in this chapter for ideas on how to increase the "you gets."

Finally, I resolved to make sure the food was there *on time* for the next day's break. As early as the 1930s, psychologist Gregory Razran discovered the "luncheon technique" (Decialdini, 1984). He found that audiences became fonder of people and things that they experienced while they were eating. Razran's subjects were presented with political statements that they had previously rated. In the second rating, only certain ones gained in approval: those presented while food was being eaten. This was an unconscious response, because the subjects couldn't remember which statements they had seen during the food service.

On the second day the group became very responsive. And, incidentally, as a result of this workshop about three-fourths of them decided to participate in the school's peer coaching program.

Podium Humor

Humor is serious business, as any television network executive will attest. My friend John Dyer, director of the Bureau of Funny Walks, former coordinator of staff development for Calgary Schools, and now senior associate at the Institute for Intelligent Behavior, is an environmental humorologist who has taught me all I know about humor. The apprenticelike quality of my use of this information is not a measure of John's gifts but of my own early stages on the journey to mastery in this area. John is funny because he looks for humor—in fact, he describes it as a state of mind or a way of interacting with the world. And, like any skilled artist, he practices frequently. One of my favorite stories is of John alone in his car at a traffic light on his way to work, practicing some new lines, slapping the dashboard, and laughing uproariously as drivers in nearby cars looked nervously in his direction.

John's greatest gift to me, and one I hope I can adequately pass on to you, is that the best presentation humor comes not from the presenter but from the audience. Perhaps it would be slightly more correct to say it comes from interactions within an environment that the presenter sculpts and then steps inside of to watch, participate with, and enjoy.

The word *humor* actually comes to us from the Greek, where *hu* indicates "huge" and *mor* refers to "morph," or "shape,"[3] caused

[3]Don't take this too seriously! Fanciful word definitions are another form of humor, but one must be careful to alert the audience of their fabricated nature. In speaking, of course, this can be signaled with gestures, facial expressions, or intonation.

by the swelling of the abdomen as oxygen is swallowed and carbon dioxide is purged during heavy bouts of laughter. Seriously, it is well known that one of the benefits of laughter is a momentary increase in pulse and blood pressure, which then drop to a level lower than before, reaching an ideal learning state. Laughter also clears the mind, refreshing the screen on each individual's personal computer.

Getting Laughs

One of my most serious dilemmas regarding humor is that the more I read about how to create humor, the more depressed I become about my own limited abilities. I've come to the conclusion that to get any better at all, I simply have to stop reading. In fact, a major motivation for writing this chapter was the selfless belief that in passing on to you some of what I've learned, I might also ease my depression. So what follows are ideas that I'm learning about presentation humor, some of which I've read and most of which John has taught me.

John says the real goal is to create an environment for humor. Since most of us are not stand-up comics, we must become environmental architects, crafting the conditions in which humor can flourish. There are three stages for these special design considerations: before the opening, during the opening, and throughout the "bawdy" of the presentation.

- **Before the Opening**

  John advises that we establish expectations for humor through our first contact with participants. For example, if the written announcement of the presentation or the signs on the workshop door contain clever graphics or cute text, that can signal a lighthearted tone to participants, preparing them to anticipate a comical touch in the presentation. So can unexpected interactions before the session. Sometimes I will whisper to a small group of early arrivers, "There's a rumor going around that this is the smart table." This usually evokes laughter and some funny comments from the participants. I was joking like that once with a group in Georgia, and a woman asked me in an exaggeratedly drawn-out voice, "Tell me, is that a *genuwine* California accent?" Everybody within earshot cracked up laughing. When someone extends a handshake and says to John, "Hi, I'm glad to meet you," he may laugh and respond with, "You don't know that yet." (Without a playful smile and a twinkle in your eye, this one might backfire.) Since rapport is never made with a group but only with individuals, personal contact and light bantering before a presentation can give permission for that tone to carry over into the work period.

- **During the Opening**

The first few minutes of a presentation are important and set norms for the rest of the session. Four ways to stimulate opening humor are autobiographical comments, cartoons, synectic exercises, and fast-break statements. Here are some examples. Art Costa and I are codirectors of the Institute for Intelligent Behavior. Since that name occasionally evokes a giggle, I sometimes build on that reaction by adding that my job is to make others feel intelligent and well dressed by my mere presence. Or sometimes I reveal that I'm an empty-nester and then define that as a parent who has grown-up children who have left home (and returned), left home (and returned), etc. Many people relate to that and the group usually laughs. Another autobiographical line is to say, "I'm glad to be here. Actually, at my age, I'm glad to be anywhere." That used to get good laughs for George Burns, and increasingly, I'm discouraged to note, for me.

Humor, of course, is best directed at ourselves, not at others. By taking ourselves lightly, we can more readily communicate with others. Herb True, a professional speaker and founder of the Management Development Program at the University of Notre Dame, gives an example of self-directed humor.

> My brother is short and heavy. He uses humor effectively by explaining that when you get on an elevator with him, you better be going down. He also likes to say that it's tough to be short like he is because you can't wear cowboy boots—they cut you under the armpits. (True, 1995).

Transparency cartoons are good laugh-getters. (Always get permission to use published work from newspapers or other sources.) I've found that covering the caption until people have absorbed the picture and then reading the caption aloud as it is displayed increases the laughter.

Synectic exercises can tap creativity and tickle the funny bone. Pairs or trios might be asked to answer the question, "What game are you playing in this organization?" The answers can get an audience roaring. "We're playing badminton in a hurricane," or "Parcheesi, because the name sounds really interesting even though we don't really know how to play it," or "Hide-and-seek, because no one ever knows what the goals are: they keep changing so frequently."

Finally, fast-break statements like "We promise to adjourn promptly at the scheduled time of 4:30" (the real ending time is 3:00) surprises people with the unexpected final thought and alerts people that you are encouraging a playful atmosphere.

- **Throughout the "Bawdy" of the Presentation**

Energizers are frequently valued by participants, particularly in long sessions. Bruce Wellman, my Vermont-based partner in The Adaptive Schools work, and I will frequently engage a group in singing "My Bonnie Lies over the Ocean," during which they shift between standing or seated positions whenever the *B* sound is sung. Silly instructions lighten moods. Sometimes we will designate, as the reporter in small-group activities, the person who is wearing the most elaborate shoes. We work to sprinkle funny lines into our most serious content.

For longer workshops, when John Dyer wishes to help people loosen up, he may get them on their feet doing something silly. "Humorobics" is one form that this can take. John explains that humorobics are uncomplicated laughing activities. He will model and invite people to (1) yawn and get ugly; (2) put both feet flat on the floor; shake the right hand and say EEEEEEEEE; shake the left arm and say AAHHHHHHH; shake the left leg and say BL-BL-BL-BL (i.e., blow through the lips); shake the right leg and say BLAAGGHHH; lift both feet off the floor and say OUCHHHH; (3) force laughter in unison, HA, HA, HA, HA, HA, HA, and continue until everyone is laughing naturally. Another exercise John does is to have a "laugh-off." Everyone forces themselves to laugh wholeheartedly and listen to everyone else's laugh as they do so. This frequently becomes uncontrollable. Wow!

A word about the title of this section. *Bawdy* as a play on the spelling of the *body* of a speech is all right, but bawdy in tone is not. While occasionally a double entendre will emerge spontaneously from either you or the audience and everyone has a hearty laugh, my experience is that deliberate comedy based on sexual innuendo is not okay. The line between good taste and barn jokes is in many shades of gray, depending on the perception of the listener. Be cautious not to offend.

How to Increase Your Humor Quotient

Presenters get better at facilitating laughter in three ways: developing knowledge and repertoire about humor, practicing, and developing a humorous state of mind.

Here are some tips for increasing comic knowledge and repertoire. Read books about humor, like Steve Allen's *How To Be Funny* (1987), read comedy books or the joke sections in *Reader's Digest,* scan the newspapers and magazines looking for cartoons that are relevant to your presentation topics, remember accidentally funny lines that emerge in your presentations, and watch comedians on TV. Many serious students of humor (Is that an oxymoron?) are subscribers to sources that serve speakers. For example:

- The Executive Speaker, (513)294-8493
- The American Speaker, (202)337-5980
- Contemporary Comedy, (214)381-4779
- Jokes Unlimited, Don Wolf, (213)876-0830
- Quote, Tom Kelly, (505)527-0381
- Laughter Prescription, (818)886-7940

One of my favorite comics is Steven Wright, whose humor is dry, unexpected, and zany. One bit I've borrowed from him is to walk across the stage, stop suddenly, take off my glasses, stare at them and say, "What do you know! My prescription just ran out!"

As in any skill development, knowledge is not enough. Practice teaches timing and refinements and contributes to unconscious competence, in which the funny line or gesture is expressed by you without conscious thought. Off-stage is as good a place as any (and safer) to experiment with comedy.

Finally, acquiring a playful state of mind is the most powerful self-development strategy. You probably have experienced times in which humor came naturally. It's likely that you just saw the comedy in the events around you and took things less seriously. We can all enter this pleasant state of lightness, either by willing it to be so or asking ourselves the question, "If there were something funny about this, what might it be?" To enter this state gets easier with practice, and the journey is smoothed by setting one's ego aside and not worrying about looking foolish or failing to get a laugh. Jim Huge, a Colorado-based consultant and master of presentation humor, taught me to say, "That's humor!" after saying anything that fails to get a laugh. As professional comics know, that sort of poking fun at one's own failed attempts does produce laughter. Probably the core and real gift of John Dyer's humor is that he never tells a joke at someone else's expense, and he reveals himself through his humor to be a genuinely caring and gentle man.

Speaking to Parents and Other Audiences

Recently a woman came up to me at the end of a presentation and said, "Thank you for speaking in a language I could understand. I'm a community representative on my school district's strategic planning commission, and often I go home after a meeting wondering just what it was the educators were talking about." Her comment caused me to reflect on the changing sea of school work and a rich learning experience that I had had with parent members of school advisory committees the week before. Both perspectives reminded me that educational jargon belongs in the faculty room and not in public meetings.

Many North American schools are being tossed on the waves of two currents on the educational horizon. One is the emerging reality that parents are partners in the school enterprise. Parent participation in school site committees has increased, and community members at large are taking greater part in public meetings, councils, and task forces. The second current is about changing demographics, spurred by an unprecedented immigration wave from all over the world. Public school classrooms—particularly in the Canadian provinces of British Columbia and Ontario and in states such as California, Florida, Texas, and New York—are filled with a rainbow of races, hundreds of different ethnic, cultural, and national groups, and the sounds of nearly a hundred different languages. Into this milieu steps the educator, presenting to increasingly mixed adult audiences.

Here are several ideas for clear speaking on complex topics, leaving "educanese" at home and making it unnecessary in public meetings.

Slow Down

Recently I conducted a two-day seminar for school advisory groups in which half of the audience was parents, some spoke no English, and many were from low-income homes. Because in any group one feels resourceful only to the degree that one is familiar with the topic, it is important to judiciously pace the flow of ideas on complex topics. I realized that in this setting of parents and educators, my typical speaking pace needed to be altered. Presenters have lots of ways they can slow the flow and make the content more user-friendly. These include speaking more slowly than usual at the beginning of a session so that participants can get used to your speech patterns and style, pausing more frequently and for longer periods, consciously using nonverbals to illustrate concepts, paraphrasing oneself, and repeating key ideas.

Enunciate

Unfamiliarity with sounds and patterns of a speaker's language can contribute to miscommunication. If many audience members speak English as a second language, learn to enunciate clearly the sounds that are unusual in languages other than English. Stephanie Nickerson (1995) notes that people whose native languages lack sounds such as the *th* in *then* and the *th* in *thin* typically substitute a *z* or *d* sound for the *th* in *then* and an *s* or *t* for the *th* in *thin*. She writes that her French-Swiss grandmother used to say, "zeeze leetle seengz zat confuse me" (these little things that confuse me). Such substitutions can make communication difficult.

Teach Vocabulary

Presenters can also teach vocabulary that has special meaning and is central to a session by alerting the audience that you will be talking about a word, using the word, defining it, giving an example, and perhaps eliciting a choral repeat of the word if it is unusual enough. For example, when working with the concept of "adaptivity," one can say, "I am going to talk about adaptivity. It is the first goal for your school improvement efforts. I will describe *what* the word means, *why* it is important, and *how* your school can attain it. To be adaptive means to change form but maintain one's identity [provide two or three examples]. Now, say it with me, please, the first goal for the school is *adaptivity.*"

Request Translators

Arrange for language translators in advance. In addition, ask for a show of hands to see who else is multilingual and can assist with translations and clarifications during a presentation. Even better, create subgrouping across roles and language groups for any group activities. Mary Bailey, a staff developer in the Fresno Unified School District, told me that when she was a principal she used to conduct some of her parent meetings in Spanish and provide an English translator so that all could appreciate the energies that go toward participating in a meeting conducted in another language.

Resist the Tendency to Consider Differences Inferior

Anthropologist Edward Hall notes that Americans have a tendency to consider differences inferior. Studies also reveal that many Americans have a tendency to unconsciously judge people who speak nonstandard English as less trustworthy and less intelligent. Nothing could be further from the truth than this assumption of limitation. I will always remember a graduate student in one of my university classes who opened his strongly accented presentation to classmates with this statement: "Please because I do not speak good English, do not consider me not smart. Remember that I am speaking to you in my second language, and I speak two others as well."

Beware the Hidden Cultural Chasms

Cultural differences aren't just about relative wealth, skin color, or national origin. Culture has to do with how one thinks about work and life. Forms of reasoning may be nationally influenced or patterned after work experiences. For example, the Aristotelian mode of reasoning that is prevalent in the West is not shared by people in Asia. Workers in an engineering firm are likely to approach problem solving differently than many teachers do. A superintendent whose total work history had been in private industry told me that six months after being hired to lead a school district, he came to appreciate the differences between education and the private sector. "We do the same work," he said, "but we live in different worlds." He explained that the social, political, and financial fabrics of the two worlds were as different as night and day, and that this led to work domains driven by different assumptions and peopled by different human resources.

Remember That Parents Are Partners

I think the popular metaphor of parents as clients may be doing us some harm. As Thomas Sergiovanni, Lillian Radford: Professor of Education and Administration at Trinity University, San Antonio, Texas reminds us, schools are not businesses, armies, or fast-food chains. Schools are closer to families (i.e., functional ones) or communities than they are to these formal organizations. Educators need their own metaphors of leadership and must stop borrowing from the private sector those which are inappropriate for schools. Consider the parent-as-client metaphor.

How does one work with a client? One has a service or a product to sell. One seeks to satisfy needs and interests, conducts polls and information surveys, and reveals some (but not all) information about the operation. One assumes a position of superiority regarding knowledge, expertise, and intention.

But relationships with partners are different. We *jointly* define intentions, set goals, discuss problems, search for resources, and own the challenges and the successes. Educators don't know *more* than parents; we know *different* things. Remembering this can help us speak beyond "educanese" when we present.

Maintaining Momentum

Notes from a Safari Journal

We started at the break of dawn today and went non-stop till midafternoon. At one point I realized I was nodding off. How was that possible? The Land Rover bounces, lurches, and jostles its way across the plains; my right hand grips a handle high over the door in the back seat. I struggle to stay alert, yet my eyes close involuntarily and I drift toward sleep. A hard bounce. My eyes open. I glance toward Sue. She too is nodding off. Somehow, Juma has kept us on the run all day, every moment an adventure, until at last we are exhausted.

I reviewed my notes for the four-hour presentation that was due the next day. Working on a yellow pad, I carefully designed graphics and selected words to describe the few process events I planned to include. The next morning I would transfer them to acetate or chart paper.

This final attention to detail can make the difference between a premier presentation and a second-rate one. Why?

Experienced presenters, like skilled train engineers, keep passengers steadily moving toward a final destination. Since it takes less energy to keep a train rolling than to start it again, certain preparation strategies and en route procedures are important to a good trip and a smooth ride. Presenters use certain procedures to maintain this comfortable momentum for individual passengers and the group.

To maintain a learning momentum for an audience, three questions must be addressed: (1) At what points can I anticipate the train might slow down? (2) How do I know when it is slowing down? (3) What can I do to either prevent loss of speed or provide sudden acceleration? While the final question is considered during the design stage, the first two are dealt with in the moment during delivery.

Anticipating

Several hills, tunnels, or turns exist that can predictably slow the train down without proper preparation. Transitions, unclear directions, elicitations, and break-time returns are some of these. Premier presenters develop preventive routines to deal with these potentially momentum-breaking situations.

- **Transitions**

  The speaker should link the past with the present, the present with the future, and all three with why the audience is there in the first place.

  Transitioning from one topic or activity to the next may lose participants' focused attention when they struggle to make connections from what happened to what is about to occur. Jon Saphier, of Research for Better Teaching, masterfully prevents this by frequently providing "train schedules" in his presentations.

  > We've just examined things teachers do to check whether students are with them or confused. Next, we are going to watch a videotape to see which of these things are going on. Then, this afternoon, we will look at the broader picture—what teachers do to keep students with them. From all of this, you will become a better observer and commenter on these aspects of instructional management.

  In this example, the speaker links past, present, and future, and all three with why the audience is there in the first place. The passengers need not worry about which stop they are at and which station is coming next.

- **Unclear Directions**

  Unclear directions can make people feel stupid. Once that happens, it takes an enormous amount of energy to get the train chugging confidently down the track again. Any preparation time to make directions clear, explicit, and elegant (minimum words, maximum understanding) pays handsomely. Graphics help.

- **Eliciting Audience Responses**

  Another problem area is how to record elicited audience responses. This occasionally can cause deadening time lags. Ask yourself, "Do I have a purpose in recording this?" If the answer is yes, recruit one, two, or more recorders from the audience to chart audience comments while you stay engaged with the group and keep the train rolling.

- **Break-Time Returns**

  Sometimes another unscheduled delay occurs after a break or a lunch period. The presenter can prepare audiences before the break for what is to follow and privately rehearse the opening statement during the break so that minimum strokes and maximum movement can be maintained. Sometimes I gather the on-timers around me after lunch and weave topic-related yarns as "icing" for them. This also serves as a reminder to late-comers that these sessions start exactly when announced. (The next section elaborates on this technique.) Another strategy is to display a brief series of contextually appropriate cartoons immediately after a break. The bursts of laughter will draw people from the hallway into the room like a friendly magnet.

Sensing the Slow-Down

Many presenters miss the subtle, and sometimes not-so-subtle, cues that the audience has already left or is leaving. (My dear friend and accomplished speaker Art Costa once had an entire audience all rise and leave an hour before the end of his presentation as part of a labor action! Out of respect for Art, and probably with some embarrassment about the planned event, they alerted him beforehand that this was going to happen.)

Presenters who sense the train slowing down do so in a variety of ways. A physical reaction is often my first alert. Something just *feels* wrong! When this occurs, I search for visual cues to confirm or explain the feeling. Blank faces, side conversations, doodling, purse packing and paper stacking are some of these. Other presenters rely on auditory cues to monitor purposeful activity in a group. They listen for the natural rhythm in a pattern of surges and rests that occur when people are working in buzz groups. Whenever the pattern is interrupted, a rest comes inappropriately in the rhythm, or the volume gets unpredictably high or low, it may signal that momentum has been lost. At that point, presenters gather visual information about what is wrong and how they might intervene. Those with keen auditory acuity learn from experience that certain activities have distinctive sound patterns. In brainstorming, for example, volume dips as people reach the stage where the group experiences a natural slowing of ideas. This is usually followed by a fresh line of thinking, more ideas, and a rise in the noise level.

Why do some presenters sense momentum shifts more readily than others? This probably has to do with how much they allow themselves to check in and out from an egocentric state of speaking to an allocentric perspective of seeing, hearing, and feeling the presentation from the audience's perspective. The ability to be sensitive to momentum shifts may also be related to a presenter's ability to keep foremost in his or her mind the goals and plan of the presentation.

Taking Action

When what you are doing is not working, change it. This simple adage eloquently applies to jump-starting the train back into motion. Do *anything* differently, even if what you are currently doing "always" holds audience interest and attention. Pick up the pace, call for buzz groups, tell a story, take a break, or restate the purpose of the current topic or activity. Here is an example of how far you might go in changing what is not working. One Thursday morning late in the school year I found myself presenting to a group of administrators who looked and acted like zombies. I adopted a rag-doll, head-sagging stance and said to them, "This is what you look like. What's going on?" I learned that yesterday they had passed out reduction-in-force notices to their teachers and that this was the fourth morning this week they had been in meetings away from their buildings. "What *should* our agenda be this morning, then?" I asked. They told me and we completely shifted gears.

Awake and Learning after Lunch

Even a ten-minute talk includes at least a thousand words. When those thousand words are directed at audience members right after lunch, the combination of full stomachs, midday fatigue, and lunch-topic diversions can potentially convert the sound of the speaker's voice to something akin to the drone of lazy afternoon flies and sleepy lullabies.

Presenters may encounter this concern in three types of after-lunch presentations: the banquet speech, the workshop that begins at 1:00 P.M., and the presentation that is a continuation of a session that began in the morning. While this chapter focuses on the third type, several of these ideas are also applicable to the first two.

There are at least three issues that presenters encounter in getting a workshop restarted after lunch: (1) stragglers, (2) post-lunch blahs, and (3) contextualizing.

Stragglers

Bruce Wellman and I anguished over this problem in a ten-day training program that was scheduled over eighteen months with bright, competent, overworked, and busy staff developers in a major U.S. city. There were two approaches we could use: be flexible and cope with the situation, or help the group change its norms. Ultimately we did both.

We hit upon the idea of offering a special (but unessential to skills development) learning dessert for persons who returned on time after lunch. We developed several criteria for these desserts. First, they were yummy, with the capacity to captivate, focus, and physically bring the audience together. Second, they were related to the topic of study. Third, they added new depth, nuances, special perspectives, or understanding to the topic. Finally, the knowledge was not essential for the entire group to be able to complete the balance of the afternoon's learning tasks.

Stories nicely meet these four criteria. Lunch time frequently found Bruce and I taking inventory of our repertoire of stories to find an appropriate one for the post-lunch session. Now I plan these in advance.

Physically arranging the seating for story time adds to the focusing effect of the story and provides a sense of intimacy and specialness for the group. I often invite the on-timers to bring their chairs forward to create an informal storytelling circle. Latecomers are drawn to the hushed atmosphere of the group and seat themselves on the periphery, sometimes encouraged by an inviting wave of my hand. When the majority of persons are present, I can segue into the afternoon's agenda.

The simple act of starting on time, regardless of how many are in the room, helps develop on-time starts as expected behavior. But group norms run deep, and sometimes more direct approaches are necessary. Whether Bruce and I are presenting Cognitive Coaching,sm group facilitation skills, or presentation skills, we routinely hold a simple "pluses and wishes" evaluation session with participants at the end of the day. With the ten-day training group I am describing, lots of comments showed up in the "wishes" section on the third day, indicating that they desired more modeling and skills practice. Bruce and I used this information to engage the group in problem solving. Without any judgment or blame, we described the start-time behavior pattern of the group, which was creating less total time together for learning. The next morning (for morning starting times were also a problem), the entire group was there on time. One person even confided, "You know, this is the first time I've *ever* been on time for anything in my life!" From that time on, the norm for the group became punctuality, despite their continuing heavy and unpredictable demands from outside.

The Post-Lunch Blahs

Frank Koontz of the Bureau of Education and Research, an organization that delivers more than 400 days of training to teachers per year, tells me that the first period after lunch is the most difficult for participants and presenters. He advises that the afternoon break be scheduled no later than one hour into the session. Since pulse rates slow significantly after about twelve minutes of sitting, any physical activities that can be appropriately included in the afternoon presentation make good sense. I use a number of interactive patterns that get people talking and/or moving. Some of these are: (1) partners take inventory and compare notes; (2) partners take turns summarizing; (3) participants get up, select a new partner, and begin a new activity together; and (4) individuals move to different corners of the room to express an opinion and, once there, tell a neighbor their rationale for making that choice.

As one speaker puts it, if adults sit too long they will "smush" (sit on) their intelligence. To prevent this from happening, lots of movement is encouraged. The walk-around survey is an excellent device for stimulating brain cells and learning. In this strategy, participants interview at least six other persons in the room, collecting three recalls and three insights from the day's work to date. This takes about five minutes and is gratefully received by participants at starting time or thirty minutes or so into the afternoon session.

Contextualizing

So it's 1 P.M. People attending the workshop have enjoyed lunch and are now settling into their seats for the afternoon session. What is most prominent in their minds is the over-lunch conversations, not the teaching points that seemed so engaging that morning. The presenter's task is to overcome inertia, refocus the group, and make connections between what occurred in the morning, the point of reentry, and the participant's own interests and goals.

One device for this is the *cliff hanger*. Just like the old Saturday afternoon movie serial that ended with the hero in some precarious position, the presenter closes the morning session with a verbal tease for the afternoon. "And what single, simple strategy can teachers use to get a 300 to 700 percent improvement in student performance (Rowe, 1986)? *That's* the question we'll address immediately after lunch!" After lunch, the presenter says, "As you will recall, this morning we explored ways to increase student participation in class. We identified three and suggested there was one more which has been shown to produce as much as a 300 to 700 percent performance improvement. Please turn to your neighbor, recall this morning's three strategies, and share what you think the next might be." This activity bridges participants' morning learning with the afternoon's focus and can also help with the straggler issue if people are not *too* late getting back.

Another strategy that accomplishes this is *paired verbal fluency*. In this approach, persons are paired; A speaks to B for one minute, telling B everything he or she has remembered from the morning. B then speaks to A for a minute. This pattern repeats for two or three cycles, each time getting just a bit shorter. I will usually position myself at the rear of the room during this activity so I can catch latecomers as they enter and direct them immediately into the activity.

Naturally, many of these strategies for dealing with after-lunch stragglers, blahs, and contextualizing are also useful at the beginning of the morning and/or at midmorning or afternoon breaks. So is humor. Songs or camp games can produce this. As described in the section on humor, singing "My Bonnie Lies over the Ocean," and shuttling between seated and standing positions at every *B* sound in the song, evokes laughter, adrenaline, and energy to carry into the next learning task.

Signaling Your Most Important Points

A well-known educational consultant used to give audiences "research" findings that claimed that at any time during a presentation, 15 percent of the audience was gone, thinking erotic thoughts. "That," he would say, "is one of the reasons I like to speak. I enjoy watching people have a good time!" While I can't locate the research base this consultant used in his assertion about audience attentiveness, there is much evidence to support his general thesis: A certain percent of the time, a certain percent of the audience will be following its own thoughts and not attending to the speaker's message. The problem that speakers have is knowing how to break through these reveries to get the major points heard by everyone. An important fact to understand

about attention is that very little is under voluntary control. People in an audience cannot make themselves listen. Attention is automatically switched off by repetitive stimuli. For example, if you are in a room with a clock that is ticking quietly, you will soon habituate to the sound, so that after a while you no longer "hear" it. But the sound is still being heard by the brain, and if the clock were to suddenly change volume, stop, or speed up, it would be noticed. Good presenters know this and vary their speed, volume, rate of ideas, and other factors to help keep people alert.

Following are eight specific strategies that do this. (see Figure 3.2). They are all based on two notions. First, the speaker has a few key points that are essential to be heard. If those points are missed, people may feel shortchanged. That is because they *would* be shortchanged if they left without knowledge of some critical assumptions, steps in a process, cautions, statements of purpose, or other points essential to getting value from the presentation. Second, audience members may need, and even appreciate, some sort of signaling system that tells them when to tune out their inner thoughts and tune in to the speaker.

1. Say, "Here is my most important point!"
2. Use silence before big ideas.
3. Move. Become a visual paragraph.
4. Speak through an imaginary megaphone.
5. Echo it. Echo it. Echo.
6. Number ideas.
7. Use physical signals.
8. Ask for choral repeats.

Figure 3.2: How to Keep People Tuned In

Eight Strategies To Keep The Audience Tuned In

1. Here Is My Most Important Point

Ed Wohlmuth has written a short and readable book on presenting, *The Overnight Guide to Public Speaking* (1983). He identifies six signals that audiences want to hear. "Here is my most important point" is one of these. Wohlmuth suggests sending this message in two parts because it takes a moment for people to leave their inner thoughts and rejoin the speaker. An example: "If you don't take anything else away from my talk today, I hope you'll remember this one point [signal]. It is, in fact, the key thought [reinforcing signal] that I came here to deliver."

2. Periods Of Silence

Employing an extended period of silence before making a point will also return people from personal trances and focus their curiosity on what is about to be said. Speakers who do not pause enough (or long enough) may sound subordinate, says Iain Ewing (1994). He reports on a study that analyzes the speech patterns of prominent French politicians, such as President François Mitterand. The findings? The more prominent the speaker, the more slowly he or she speaks, and with more and longer pauses. Figure 3.3 displays some interesting data that seem to support this point. I don't know of similar studies with English speakers, but my memory of speeches by very powerful persons—Maya Angelou, Winston Churchill, Martin Luther King, Jr., and John F. Kennedy, for example—all reinforce this concept.

Person and context of speech	Percentage of pause time in speech	Average length of pause
1974, Mitterand as opposition politician running for president	30%	0.8 seconds
1984, Mitterand at the peak of his power as a popular president of France	45%	2.1 seconds

Figure 3.3: Power Pausing

3. Visual Paragraph

Becoming a visual paragraph will also help audience members tune in. This is television jargon for moving with deliberate silence to some new spot on the platform. This alerts an audience that something different is going to be said. Take advantage of the many natural transitions in your presentation by signaling these changes with your position in the room:

- after your introduction and as you start the body of your speech;
- as you move from your first main point to your second;
- as you pause to listen to a question, then move to answer it;
- as you move from the body of your work into your conclusion.

4. Megaphone

Speaking through a megaphone is also effective at getting the audience to tune in. Since I don't own one, I sometimes cup my hands on either side of my mouth to speak. Like a human megaphone, I lower my voice and boom out a statement. Because this signaling procedure lacks the two parts that Wohlmuth describes as necessary for audience members, I often combine this with the next strategy.

5. Echo

Echo. I will simply say it again; same phrasing, same intonation. I've found the echo to be an effective strategy, with or without the megaphone.

6. Numbers

Numbers also capture people's attention. Occasionally I use them to create advance organizers and focus attention. "Now there are three important things to keep in mind during implementation. Number one [said with inflectional stress] is..." I'm always amazed at how many people will reach for a pencil when I start this pattern.

7. Other Physical Signals

Numbers can be combined with visual paragraphing. Number one (the speaker makes a point and then moves to a new location). Number two (the speaker makes the next point), and so on. Numbers can also be combined with other physical signals, such as raised fingers. In fact, the more the presenter speaks simultaneously to the right and left sides of the brain, the more potently and clearly the signals are received.

8. Choral Repeats

Playfully engaging the audience in choral repeats will also bring focused attention to key points.

There are, of course, other strategies; but I think that what you will discover, whatever the strategy, is that the most effectively delivered important points are sent as "soundbytes." These are brief information capsules that can be received, recorded, and repeated by persons reared in a television era. Analysts say that speaking in soundbytes became a potently effective communication strategy in the 1988 presidential election (Noonan, 1990). In that year, the average length of a candidate's statement on evening network news was 9.8 seconds. Twenty years earlier, the average was 42.3 seconds, and in 1992, the last year for which I have data, it shrunk to an incredibly brief 7.3 seconds (see Figure 3.4). If the sentence is so long that you have to take a breath, it may be too long for your audience to understand. Keep it short.

Year	Average Length of Candidate's Statement Broadcast on Evening Network News
1968	42.3 seconds
1988	9.8 seconds
1992	7.3 seconds

Figure 3.4: The Shrinking Soundbyte

Teaching on Triple Tracks

Like the experience with the hippo in Ngorongoro Crater, some experiences in a seminar room can be painful and also be a source of learning. It was immediately following a presentation at a national conference that Bruce Wellman and I first realized the extraordinary usefulness of teaching on triple tracks. While scanning the post-session participant evaluations, we were stung by one in particular. According to this person's experience, we had been abstract, vague, theoretical, and our work had lacked utility because of the absence of concrete examples. We were stunned by the anger in the participant's language. He had given us his valuable time and was going away empty-handed. And we were

Notes from a Safari Journal

Not all learning is pleasant. It is late morning. I've been drinking coffee. I step cautiously from the safari vehicle to adjust the balance between my fluid intake and outgo. Suddenly from behind me appears a hippopotamus—the animal responsible for more human deaths than any other on the African continent. He, she, or it is enormous (we decide it's a she), with canines up to eighteen inches long. The guidebook says this one weighs somewhere between 4,000 and 7,000 pounds. Grunting and snorting, glistening and terrifying, she comes charging directly at me from the waterhole from which she emerged. Sue and Juma are yelling for me to get back in the vehicle. The hippo is oblivious to us, our noise, our fear. I get in. We grab cameras and click, click, click, our shutters record her as she slips into the muddy water to our side.

also puzzled, because we thought we had designed the presentation with specificity, examples, and applications in mind.

Our reflection led us to two hypotheses: (1) the writer was a concrete sequential processor in the extreme, and (2) something had happened in our opening that interacted with his perceptions in such a way that he missed the concrete portions of the presentation and focused only on that which was conceptual. With this in mind, Bruce and I began deliberately tuning and refining a process that he and Laura Lipton had intuitively begun to use when they presented together.

We call this approach *triple-track presenting*. Its benefits include satisfying a range of learning styles, transfering learning to a range of applications, assisting memory, and making a public record of the interactive strategies used in a presentation. If you'd like to test this approach in your own presentations, here are some ideas to get you started.

Setting the Stage

During your opening invite the audience to attend to certain experiences at three levels. First, advise them that you will use interactive learning strategies that are designed to support their learning throughout this seminar. You will comment on the rationale and the intended contribution of each of these strategies to their learning. Second, explain how each strategy might also be adapted for classroom work with students. At the third level,

First Track	• Use a learning activity to support group learning. • Post the name of the activity on butcher paper on the wall. • Describe the learning theory being employed. • Describe conditions under which it would and would not be appropriate.
Second Track	• Give examples of how the same activity can be used in classrooms to support student learning.
Third Track	• Give examples of how the same activity can be modified to support groups in faculty meetings, curriculum committee work, site based decision-making groups, etc.

Figure 3.5: Presenting on Three Tracks

you will describe how the same processes can be used to support other adults with whom these participants might work.

Next, post a chart labeled "Strategies." Hang it high on a wall so that it maintains visual prominence throughout the presentation. Each time you engage the audience in an interactive learning process, name the process, write it on the strategy chart, give origins and a pedagogical rationale for the strategy, and describe specific ways to apply the strategy with other adults and with students.

Model the Process at Your First Opportunity

You can begin to use this process in the opening of a presentation. Here is an example.

> In just a moment we are going to engage in an inclusion activity. On page __ of your handout you'll find a section to record ideas. You may wish to take some notes there regarding the purposes of inclusion activities and some specific inclusion strategies you can use in meetings, seminars, or with students.

> Give the rationale for the strategy.

> Inclusion strategies typically serve these purposes. They: (1) help people know who they are in relation to the entire group, (2)

> focus the group's mental energy inside the room, (3) establish a norm of participation, and (4) begin the journey from "me-ness" to "we-ness"—the progression toward interdependence.
>
> The inclusion strategy we will use to help you get a sense of who is here today is called "like me." In a moment, I will make some statements. For each statement that is like you, stand, look around, and see who else fits that particular category.

Some generically useful categories for the like-me strategy are roles, time in a district, the state one was born in, up before 6 A.M., experience with the topic, and a passion for chocolate. Be sure to include "other" as a role category. Persons left out at this stage will often feel unacknowledged for some time into the seminar.

Now give specific examples of how the like-me strategy can be used in other settings, such as parent meetings, at beginning-of-the-year faculty assemblies, in other seminars, or with students. As much as I would like the transfer of ideas to be automatic without my giving specific examples, for most persons it seems not to occur.

David Perkins and Gavriel Salomon (1991) suggest that presenters facilitate transfer when they provide proximal or distal bridging. *Proximal bridging* involves giving examples in which the new situation so closely approximates the situation in which the learning occurred that the application is fairly obvious. In this case, we've used the like-me strategy in a seminar, then described how it might be used by these participants as they conduct their own seminars with other groups. *Distal bridging* refers to more distant, remote, or obscure applications (Costa, 1991), in which the elements are greatly dissimilar to those in which the skill or concept has been learned. With the like-me strategy, this might include descriptions of applications at a parents' back-to-school night or examples of changing the text of the like-me statements to fit a special circumstance. For example, in a community forum gathered for problem-solving purposes, statements such as "I have more than three solution suggestions," "I have an idea from which I will not budge," "I know someone in another school who has a successful resolution," "I'm willing to explore options but I don't think some of my neighbors are," might be used in place of the more generic inclusion statements. To provide proximal or distal bridging examples adds another level of detail to your preparation work. It also multiplies the usefulness of your work by about three times, however.

For each strategy you use, you can choose to add to the group's repertoire other strategies that would accomplish similar aims. For example, you might describe other inclusion activities and record their names on the public strategy list. In "Peter Paul," two people interview each other, then introduce their partner to the group. "Cash Flow" is another inclusion activity and mixer in which everyone gets money (Monopoly) at the door. The task is to look for people with whom all money adds up to a predetermined amount, and form groups. However, since transfer is generally enhanced when learning has been constructed out of personal experience, these described strategies may not transfer as well as the experienced ones.

There is one unexpected benefit of triple-track presenting for the presenter: It requires us to be more articulate about why we are choosing particular learning strategies. I know I feel pressed to expand my repertoire. One idea for repertoire expansion is to take inventory of one's own frequently used processes to support adult learning. Reflect on why they are used, what is known about principles of learning that supports their use, and what other strategies might be used or invented that could produce similar learning benefits.

Some Strategy Examples

Here are a few dependable standbys:

- **AB Each Teach**

  To support participants in internalizing technical information, have them randomly pair off. In a standing conversation, A teaches B a portion of content just covered as if B had not been in the room. B then teaches A another portion of content. This strategy is useful not only as a review, but also supports learners in constructing a language with which to tell others about the topic. It also creates an energy surge for participants.

- **Touch Red**

  I learned this strategy from Gale Mills, an extraordinary staff developer from Texas. It's great for energizing groups in settings where people have been together for a little while. It is used to regroup participants and acknowledge special roles within the group.

  The presenter asks persons to "touch red," meaning to locate a person wearing that color and touch them anywhere that is appropriate—the hand or arm, for example. Emphasize that it is not necessary to touch them directly *on* the color, but that they must directly touch the person, not someone else who is touching the person.

  Now use some other categories. Touch blue, or a principal, or a kindergarten teacher, or someone who's worked in the district twenty years or more, or a grandparent. After four to eight regroupings, ask each person to select someone standing next to them to be their learning partner for the next piece of work and to sit together.

- **3-2-1**

  This is an excellent review activity. Ask individuals to record three recollections from the previous instruction, two observations (about themselves, the topic, or the group), and one insight. Provide about five minutes of silence for individual writing and review of notes. Now ask trios to share their data searching for patterns. This activity may be extended for diagnostic and instructional purposes by asking for a few reports of observations and insights. A variation on this activity is to ask groups to formulate a question instead of an insight. The presenter should be prepared for a longer public processing time to address some of the questions.

- **Muscle Memory**

  I learned this first from my friend Michael Grinder, an Oregon-based consultant who teaches educators all over the world how to make teaching more effective for students. Later I discovered another source related to training IBM executives and senior management personnel. When people add muscular movement—that is, they stand and practice a movement or a phrase—the likelihood of retention and continued application over time is greatly enhanced. Grinder's genius is that he has enhanced the experiential learning by having participants practice skills the right *and* the wrong way, and then do a kinesthetic check for appropriateness. At IBM (Whitmore, 1994), the recall level for groups who were told something was 70 percent after three weeks. But recall for these groups dropped to 10 percent after three months. For groups who were told *and shown,* the three-month recall level was 32 percent; and for those who were told and shown, and then had an actual experience, the three-month recall level jumped to 65 percent. Many groups need to hear this rationale to help them overcome the self-consciousness of a muscle-memory activity and actively engage in practice.

- **Draw the Concept**

  I learned this one from John Dyer. Following an initial keynote or contextual address, participants are provided with flip-chart paper and felt-tip pens to draw what they have learned. These drawings are then presented, in groups or by individuals.

Participant Responses to Triple-Track Learning

Here are some responses I've learned to expect when using the triple-track pattern: First, in the postsession evaluations, lots of people comment on how appreciative they were of getting many concrete strategies. Partner huddling during the session is frequent, with one partner explaining a strategy to the other if the person has forgotten any details related to the strategy or has come in late and missed the experience and explanation altogether. Often participants will approach me at break time, notes in hand, asking an application question about a particular strategy. I also observe many participants visually scanning the strategy charts during reflective periods. And, periodically, both Bruce and I get requests for permission to take the charts and have them posted in staff rooms as reminders of strategies.

I haven't done any follow-up queries to learn how much is being transferred and applied several months later. Conceptually, I know this will be enhanced by the degree of modeling I provide, the opportunities in the seminar for mediated reflection on the strategies we've used, and the degree to which the organizational environment signals compatible values and provides opportunities for practice, experimentation, and application of concepts.

Using Instruments to Support Learning

When spider webs unite, they can tie up a lion.

-Egyptian Proverb

We were fifteen minutes into a three-day seminar. Each participant began to record ideas for making meetings productive on 3 x 5 cards. Participants seated at tables shared and organized their ideas by categories, then "shopped" the data at other tables to add to their information base. This simple exercise illustrates three learning concepts that are important for adult learners. First, learning is accelerated by having participants make connections to prior information. Second, knowledge is actively constructed by learners rather than being passively received from the environment. Third, instruments—in this case, 3 x 5 cards—have an important role in supporting knowledge retrieval and construction.

Activating and Engaging Prior Learning

I've learned from colleagues Laura Lipton and Bruce Wellman that a surefire way to support adults in accelerating their learning and helping them retain large amounts of new material is to begin instruction with an exercise that activates and engages prior learning. As illustrated in the example above with the 3 x 5 cards, this is most effective when the exercise engages the learner, not only with their own mental activity but with other learners. Such experiences tend to generate both information and the motivation to learn more. They also accelerate the retention of new information because they aid the learner in bringing information to the working memory and categorizing it. As Laura Lipton says, this "raises Velcro bristles on the brain so new information sticks" (personal communication, 1995). In the classroom, such activities also level the playing field—students learn from one another—and bring misconceptions about a topic to the surface. Such activating experiences are part of a larger construct, that of constructivism.

Teachers Construct Learning, Too

Professional development programs are enhanced when they are congruent with instructional and curriculum practices for students. After all, "constructivist learning theory is not age- or stage-bound but refers to the processes of cognition for humans" (Lambert, 1995). Consider a few "constructionist" premises that drive instructional practices in an increasing number of schools.

Four Premises About Learning

1. Individuals create knowledge by reflecting on their past physical and mental actions and on their current knowledge, skills, and attitudes.
2. Knowledge is an evolving conversation with one's environment, oneself, and others.
3. For learning to occur, learners must see the relevance of the knowledge and the skill in their lives.
4. Instruction does not cause learning.

Applying these premises to adult learning, we begin to see the special contributions that learning instruments can make to the construction of meaning. Like other presenters, I've been using learning instruments—surveys, self-assessments, journals—on an intuitive basis for some time. However, when they are related to understanding how learners learn, their use in presentations starts to take on special significance.

Using Learning Instruments

Instrumentation is a technique to facilitate learning through gathering data in a systematic or structured way. Not surprisingly, the first issue for the presenter who uses instruments is purpose. Several classes of learning purposes exist to which instruments make a useful contribution. These include using instruments to assess a group prior to instruction; warm up a group at the beginning of a session; activate and engage prior learning; support concept attainment; aid introspective self-asessment; generate data for diagnosis of a group; take an inventory of knowledge, strategies, and skills; and summarize and integrate learning. Following are some factors and considerations that apply most broadly to all these purposes.

Setting the Stage

Learners get the most value from an instrument when they know why it is being used, how it relates to the larger learning agenda and their jobs, its limitations (e.g., "This is a brief instrument to sample your reactions at this point in time—it is to be used only to begin a conversation"), and how it will be "processed" or "scored and interpreted" during the presentation. For most instruments, enough time needs to be provided for ninety-five percent of the participants to complete the written work. To wait for the slowest processor in the room to finish contributes to restless energy and a loss of momentum. Because learning instruments have the common purpose of bringing up data for consideration and conversation, it is rare that everyone would need to complete the written task to achieve this. Ensure respectful silence in the room so that those distracted by talking have the benefit of a quiet atmosphere.

Selecting the Instruments

Many types of learning instruments can be devised by the presenter and are relatively easy to administer. Here are a few that combine simplicity with potency.

- **Personal Inventories**
  Ask participants to list or mindmap personal attributes, such as strategies for redirecting classroom behavior, items they consider when planning a lesson, ways they establish rapport, strengths they bring to a topic, and what they wish to learn in this seminar. These inventories activate prior knowledge and can serve as a source of data for conversations in trios or quartets in which the group looks for patterns, or as data for "cross inventories" with a partner in which

each person adds to their repertoire of strategies or information.

- **Self-Report Inventories**

  These instruments are more structured and are usually researched and located by presenters rather than constructed. These tools produce information about leadership style, cognitive style, educational philosophy, and other personal attributes. They are frequently in the format of forced choice, rating scales, yes-no, or multiple choice. Scoring, interpretation, and conversations in which participants construct personal meaning are essential activities to follow the use of these instruments.

- **Feedback Devices**

  Feedback instruments are tools used by participants to collect data about the behavior of groups or other participants in skills-development sessions. Designated learners are invited to gather data while a group is practicing a skill, working on a task, or conducting a simulated meeting. These "process observers" usually work with a data-gathering form. This form might offer the following instructions: "Record the frequency of member contributions during this interchange. Also tally the frequency with which individual members paraphrase one another or ask probing question to get more information." The process observers then report the data to the group. Recently, several of us have been extending this notion with the use of "group coaches" who gather data for a group, but instead of simply reporting the information, they assume the role of a cognitive coach for the group (Costa and Garmston, 1994) and support the group in reflecting the group's effectiveness, the individual contributions to the work of the group, and the relationship of the data gathered to those two foci.

- **Conceptual Jump-Starts**

  These instruments are simple in format yet complex in construction because they require the presenter to locate the simplest possible question that will evoke the richest possible conceptual reflection. Conceptual jump-start instruments are often best administered to trios or quartets.

  Here are some examples I learned from Bill Baker at the Institute for Intelligent Behavior. "Compare inquiry with interrogation. What is the same? What is different? What are your conclusions?" And: "Compare supervision with evaluation. In what ways are they the same and different? What do you infer?"

Here is another type of example. Ask individuals to write a response to the following: "What is the most effective question you have ever been asked? [i.e., that produced the most change in your life]? What was it about it or the circumstances in which it was asked that made it so effective?" Based on this data, ask trios to develop a list of criteria for life-changing questions.

Processing Findings

The instruments you use are only as good as the quality of data processing provided. Personal inventories should be followed with conversations with colleagues in which insights are articulated and bridges are built between the personal data and the learning task of the group. Usually a minimum of ten minutes is needed for this. Longer periods for processing are required—anywhere from twenty to forty-five minutes—for more complex instruments designed as self-report, feedback devices, or conceptual jump-starts. It's often useful to ask a group to search for patterns in its responses. What were the major things that were learned? What have we learned about ourselves as a learning community?

Responding to Questions

Don't you think that if we implement this program, it's just going to cause teachers a lot more work, with no real benefits for students?

—Workshop Participant

The workshop is just thirty minutes old. The participant who is speaking seems tense. His face is strained; his voice is loud. Other participants focus intently on him. They are very interested in the presenter's response. The presenter, seemingly at ease, draws from a practiced repertoire and responds elegantly. The questioner is satisfied. The workshop moves on.

How does a presenter know how to respond to the various questions and comments by participants? I have come to some tentative conclusions as a result of reflecting on my own continuing efforts in this area, from watching master presenters with different styles, like Arthur Costa (emeritus professor from California State University, Sacramento) and Pat Wolf (independent consultant from Napa, California) and through examining the literature on response strategies and unconscious decision-making processes.

I believe some answers to this persistent question may lie in an adaptation I've made of the S.C.O.R.E. model (Dilts, 1989). The letters stand for Symptoms, Causes, Outcomes, Resources, and Ecology (see Figure 3.5). Without using these labels or being consciously aware of this particular mental map, the best presenters consider these elements before responding to a participant.

I'll define the terms in Figure 3.6 in the sequence in which they are likely to occur in the presenter's mind.

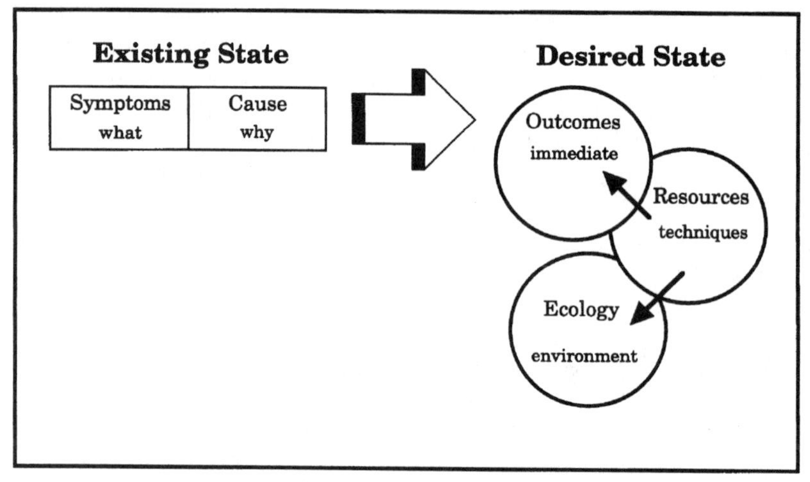

Figure 3.6 S.C.O.R.E. Model

- **Symptoms** *An audience member comments.* In applying the S.C.O.R.E. model, I'm treating what is said as a symptom, a surface manifestation of something deeper. Any question or remark is viewed as symptomatic of some participant experience, perception, concern, or thought. These stimuli begin the following thought processes.
- **Causes** *Why this question, from this person, at this time?* This is the "why" behind the participant's original question. I am not exactly aware of how I consider this in selecting an outcome and response. My hunch is that while I always intuitively think about it, I only consciously put energy here when strong emotional signals accompany the question. In these cases, I strive to tune my acuity to the speaker so finely that I can make adjustments in the second half of my sentence based on the feedback I receive from the first half of my sentence.

- **Outcomes** *What outcome do I want to produce?* Having received a question or a remark from an audience member, the presenter must design a response that leads to some desired state, such as the satisfaction of a participant's curiosity, a mood of inquiry, or laughter. These outcomes may be intended for the individual participant, a subgroup, or the entire audience. This may be the most important stage of presenter thought, for without clear intentions, responses are likely to produce random, and sometimes undesirable, results. In my work, I am conscious of at least five classes of response outcomes: (1) validating data, (2) building a knowledge base, (3) shifting perspectives, (4) understanding participant thinking, and (5) extending thinking.
- **Resources** *What strategies might I use to get the results I desire?* The resources are the techniques, stories, and moves in the presenter's repertoire, remembered or spontaneous, that are called upon to reach the outcome. These response techniques may vary according to the class of outcome.

For example, presenters *validate data* when they give direct answers to questions like, "Could you give me an example?", "What is the research?", or "Who were the authors?"

To *build a knowledge base*, a presenter might give data, provide references, tell an anecdote, give an example, or affirm or correct the participant's contribution. Presenters also build knowledge by eliciting audience responses through questions like, "How do other people handle that?" or "Turn to your neighbor and list four additional strategies."

To *shift perspectives*, again an anecdote or metaphor might be appropriate. Other techniques can also be used: humor, presenting data from another person's perspective (such as a child's or a parent's), or responding at a logical level that is different from the one in which the question was asked. For example, to the question, "Why doesn't the district provide more manipulatives?", a response might be, "Here are three ways to make free manipulatives in your immediate environment." One can also provide an experience as a response.

To *understand participant thinking*, the presenter paraphrases, asks for examples, or probes for relevance, intentionality, values, metacognition, or application.

Finally, to *extend thinking,* presenters may use wait time, give content-neutral acknowledgments (such as "uh huh," "yes," "ok," or "thanks"), paraphrase, or ask for clarification, elaboration, evidence, and information about thinking processes.

- **Ecology** *What effect will my response have on the learning climate?* In selecting a response, the presenter evaluates the effect that it would have on the learning environment. If the response will (1) maintain the momentum toward meeting the workshop goals in a timely manner, (2) keep the presenter's credibility intact, (3) encourage continued responsiveness from the group, and (4) contribute to feelings of individual and group efficacy, the response is truly elegant.

So how do presenters get better at responding to questions? I have found the following three steps useful: (1) collect response strategies, (2) use personal pause time, and (3) reflect and self-assess after each presentation.

Collect Response Strategies

Be on the lookout for ways to increase your response repertoire. Here are a few ideas I've learned recently that add to my confidence and, I think, my effectiveness at answering questions.

When conducting a question-answer period after a presentation, always tell the audience there will be a ten-minute maximum for questions and answers. Recruit a timekeeper to help you stick to this time allotment. This puts the idea of brevity into the audience's mind before anyone rises to ask a question, and it decreases the chances of rambling questions.

Identify the next three people you plan to recognize. This helps people relax to participate in the conversation (I'm either next or I'm not in the queue) and also sends a signal for brevity—theirs and yours.

Listen for the syntax of a question to determine whether it is true/false ("Should we change the schedule?"), multiple choice ("Should we buy the equipment now or later?"), short answer ("How many? How much? When? Who?"), or essay ("Why should we change the schedule?"). Then answer the question in the syntax that matches the way it was presented ("Should we change the schedule?" "Yes! Here are three reasons why.") Short answers, according to research conducted by Communication Development Associates (Weiner, 1989), are more credible than long ones. CDA advises answering the question in summary form first and then elaborating.

Another strategy is to summarize the question first. Your summary does not need to be a full repetition of the question, but it does need to clarify what was asked. There are three powerful reasons for making a simple summary of a question before answering it: (1) the questioner is assured that the speaker understands the question, (2) the rest of the group can hear the question, and (3) it focuses the presenter's attention to the exact question.

If there are several questions wrapped into one, enumerate them as you respond.

I started this section with an example of a tough question to answer. "Feel, felt, found" is the strategy the speaker in this example might have used. The participant asked, "Don't you think that if we implement this program, it's just going to cause teachers a lot more work, with no real benefits for students?" The presenter might have replied, "I know just how you *feel*, because when I was first exposed to this program, I *felt* the same way. All I could see was the bookkeeping. It looked like I had to spend time learning new systems and it was going to increase my preparation time. What I've *found*, however, as I began to work with it, is that while there was some initial upfront work, my load is actually easier now, and student work has improved tremendously."

Speakers must be very careful with the first step of this response. If you don't really know how the person feels (and it's likely that you don't unless you have directly experienced it), you can't say, "I know how you feel." What *is* possible to say, however, is, "I know that many teachers feel that way when they first come into contact with the program." Another caution with this response is to keep in mind that your intent is not to persuade this person about the value of the program. Your job is to give information, to support participants in having access to the internal resources needed for learning—energy, interest, emotions—and to offer them choices.

Readers may wish to review other ideas on how to respond to questions in Robert Garmston and Bruce Wellman's book, *How to Make Presentations That Teach and Transform* (1992).

Use Personal Pause Time

The more aware that presenters are of their thinking processes while they are responding, the more focused and effective they can be at reaching outcomes. I've recently given myself permission to pause before responding. I consciously ask myself two questions, not necessarily in the following order: (1) What are the possible ways I could answer this? and (2) What's my desired state for participants (in the moment and for an ongoing ecological learning environment)? I also consider, on an intuitive level, all that I know about the group, this particular participant, and the setting in which the group is working. This helps me understand the "why" of the individual's question and tailor a response that answers the thinking behind it. My two questions, posed consciously, create a simplified map for me of a complex dynamic situation. This frees me to work straightforwardly, in an uncomplicated manner, trusting my intuition and experience to guide me in the nuances of my response.

From Michael Grinder I've learned to use a few nonverbal cues to signal the audience to allow me time to think. Being still and allowing one's gaze to fix on some distant point above is, for most of us, a thinking posture that is recognized and respected by others. Freezing a gesture, stretching out one's hand, or putting a finger by the side of one's nose all communicate to people that you need time for your own processing. Michael's advice to presenters is, "Choose a gesture that makes you look intelligent, then freeze it while you think." I will sometimes just say to a group, "Let me think about that."

Reflect and Self-Assess after Each Presentation

Any person who is too busy to reflect upon his or her work is too busy to improve.

Good teachers and presenters keep learning from their experiences in presenting. They do this by recalling what occurred, comparing their desired outcomes with the achieved outcome, self-evaluating, and mentally rehearsing other approaches. We know that athletes who mentally practice in addition to physically practicing perform better than athletes who only do the physical practice. No amount of physical practice cancels this advantage (Elgin, 1990). This is also true for presenters. The mental practice during reflection keeps presenters profiting from each experience. Even when their response strategy has not produced the results they wanted, they're able to "fail forward" (see "Taming the Content-Process Teeter-Totter," Chapter 2).

What to Do with Your Body While Your Mouth Is Moving

Body language is an extremely apt term to describe an important way in which we communicate. In the first few milliseconds of our perceiving something, we not only unconsciously comprehend what it is but decide whether we like it or not. The physiology responsible for this, in the animals we observed on safari and in humans, is the hippocampus, a part of our limbic system

Notes from a Safari Journal

The lioness's coat was smooth and tawny with whitish underparts. Her ears, white on the inside with black markings on the outside, were erect with total attention, watching the lone wildebeest, unaware, a few yards away. Her hunting companion, and perhaps sister, lay quietly in the grass, watching and waiting. We watched, barely breathing, fascinated by this drama. Down the dirt track sauntered a jackal. One look and this shaggy, wiry animal began to move like a hyperactive adolescent, scampering excitedly between the lions and the wildebeest, sensing a kill and a possible meal. The wildebeest, startled by the jackal's movement, looked up, saw the predators, and ran out of range.

that is responsible for registering and making sense of perceptual data, and the amygdala, a storehouse of emotional opinions and memories. The amygdala is connected directly to the eyes via the optic nerve. When we see something, the visual information goes first to the amygdala before it is carried to elsewhere in the brain. This is why the nonverbal communication that we express to audiences when we present is so important. In fact, in many cases, what we say with our body tells an audience whether it should or should not trust what we are saying with our words.

There are two excellent sources of information on presenters' use of nonverbal communication. One is the work of Michael Grinder (1993), who has observed more than five thousand classrooms and has noted the effect of the teacher's nonverbal behaviors on students. The second is a book I discovered while doing some work in Singapore. It's by Iain Ewing (1994) and has the most complete treatment of presentation body language I've ever encountered.

For an example of the potency of nonverbal language, imagine this scene, which I observed not long ago in a seminar with Grinder. Pairs of adults are talking about a task. The presenter speaks with a subgroup. He raises his voice to be heard over the cacophony of student voices in the room. The students' voices increase one notch in volume. The presenter, to be heard, also increases his volume. This pattern repeats. Then, within the din, the presenter stops talking, cocks his head, and listens. When he hears a lull, barely discernible to me until he points it out, he speaks again, but this time in a voice one notch lower in volume than the students. Their voices slide down. He lowers his again, so do they, and soon, without any intervention other than what I have just described, everyone in the room is talking at a whispered hush.

Grinder explains that 82 percent of classroom management messages come from nonverbal cues. By consciously being in command of one's own nonverbal cues, a presenter can maintain positive relationships with the audience while managing participants' attention, transitions, and directions with quiet ease. This, says Grinder, allows one to teach the content even more effectively.

Breathe

Fundamental to premier presenting, according to Grinder, is the art of breathing: controlling it in oneself, monitoring it in others, and influencing audience breathing to be deep, relaxing, and calming. To breathe deeply is to release calming chemicals into the bloodstream. The human brain, at a mere three to four pounds in weight, consumes 25 to 37 percent of the body's oxygen. When audience members are breathing in a high and shallow manner, their bodies are entering a stress state. Instead of preparing one for learning, this breathing pattern prepares one for fight or flight. This emotional information enters the brain via a different neural network than cognitive information does. Research is now confirming that emotions have a separate system of nerve pathways, through the limbic system to the cortex, which allows emotional signals to avoid conscious control (Ornstein, 1991). This signal separation is useful in emergencies, but it also overrides conscious impulses. It interferes with learning.

How, then, do you recognize shallow breathing? First, focus on your own experience. Recall a situation that was difficult. Stay with it a moment and reexperience it. Notice that your breathing is probably high and shallow. Now, in contrast, recall a vacation that was pleasurable. Notice your breathing. It is probably deep and slow. Both presenter and audience members should stay as much as possible with the second type of breathing to maximize their mental functioning.

There are several ways to notice when individuals are breathing shallowly. The shoulders lift, and the upper chest heaves rapidly or freezes in place. Movement becomes jerky, and language lacks fluidity and stumbles. Fillers ("um," "uh") are often present. Shock of any kind will inhibit a group's breathing: surprise; an off-color comment; a verbal attack on an individual, the group, or the presenter; or a tactless statement. When you see that a group has stopped breathing in this manner, you want to get them breathing again.

To detect when the group stops breathing deeply, look slightly over the heads of an audience. You will know that collective shallow breathing is occurring if all the heads suddenly pull back as if jerked from behind with a string. For oxygen to be available for learning, you must see those bodies relax again and their shoulders lower. The best starting place is to breathe correctly yourself. Stop, pause, breathe deeply. You may wish to step away from the spot where the frozen breathing was evoked. Now speak slowly and calmly in a low register. Another way to get a group breathing deeply again is to make them laugh; another is to make them move their bodies. It is impossible to get up, find a new partner, and sit in a new place without richly changing one's breathing patterns. My friend Suzanne Bailey uses another technique. Sometimes she just says to an audience, "Breathe!"

Wait

> *The notes I handle no better than many pianists. But the pauses between the notes—ah, that is where the art resides!*
>
> —Artur Schnabel

A potent nonverbal cue related to breathing is silence. Silence can be one of your most useful linguistic tools when making a presentation. Silence before a statement puts a spotlight on what is about to be said; silence between an attention request (please look this way) and the content separates these two messages and prepares an audience to pay attention. Three to five seconds of silence after a presenter asks a question and after a participant responds increases group dialogue and complex thinking. Since a good, full, deep breath can take anywhere from three to five seconds, presenters can use their own breathing as a stopwatch for this important presentation tool.

Short silences or pauses can also make the difference between sounding credible and rambling. Figure 3.3 showed us some surprising research that links the percent of silence in a speech and the length of a speaker's pauses with power and influence. Notice that newscasters are adept at strategically employing silence in their sentences. They also convey credibility by curling the sound down at the end of sentences. Curling up sounds like asking a question. The first is more *credible*, and the second is more *approachable*.

Choose the Right Voice

The best presenters combine breathing and pausing with a credible and an approachable voice. When giving directions, they are credible. When presenting data, they are credible. But when they wish to elicit responses, invite opinions, encourage participation, or engage in a collegial stance with the audience, they use an approachable voice. These subtle variances in voice usage also represent a key distinction between *facilitating meetings* and *conducting presentations*. Because facilitation is about helping a group make decisions, about 80 percent of the facilitator's use of voice is approachable—melodic and curling up at the end of sentences. "Who has another idea? Are you ready to move on? I think Cirenio has something to share. Where are we now in the process?" Presenting calls for an approachable voice some of the time, but more often a credible one—chin held still, tones curling down at the end of sentences, less melody. "Here are three important points. Please turn to page four. The research on this started in the 1990s."

Use Your Hands Deliberately

Iain Ewing is a Canadian with Scottish roots who has lived in Asia for many years. He believes that, even though certain hand gestures can mean different things in different cultures, there is a universal language of gestures. Here are some tips drawn from his work (1994), Grinder's work (1993), and my own observations of remarkably effective presenters.

What to avoid:

- hands behind the back and feet spread in a parade rest stance;
- the fig leaf—hands folded over the body below the waist;
- a fist—it's threatening in any language;
- the "critical parent" gesture—this is the pointing index finger;
- grooming moves—adjusting one's tie, smoothing one's hair;
- holding (and playing with) anything other than presentation notes.

What to use:

- An open, welcoming gesture, particularly at the start of your talk, communicates that you are open, confident, and friendly. Rushing the gesture ruins the message. Hold your hands out for a few seconds. How large should this gesture be? Keep two factors in

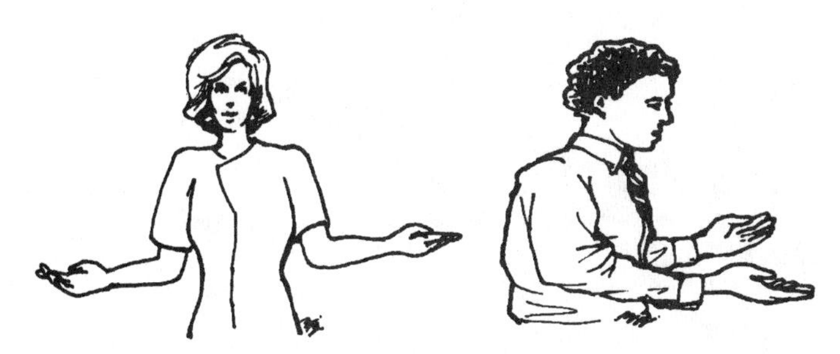

mind: (1) The larger the audience, the larger the gesture; in a small room, talking to half a dozen people, a large gesture would look ridiculous; (2) the cultural background of the audience; Asian audiences, says Ewing, are often startled by quick and large movements, so smaller gestures are in order.

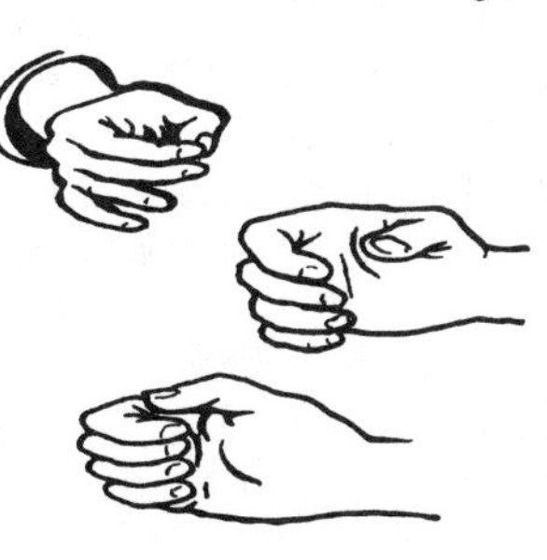

- Gestures that illustrate: Suzanne Bailey is a master at painting pictures with her hands. If she is talking about having a cup of coffee, her hands illustrate it. If she is talking about an abstraction, such as rhythm in an organization, her hands will do a hula, illustrating the concept. People will understand you better and remember more of what you say when you use gestures that illustrate.
- "Out-there" pointing: To describe negative attributes of a group of people, move to the wall and point "out there," saying that in some cases we will find people behaving that way. This protects your audience from unintentional referencing gestures you might use that would lead them to unconsciously believe you were assigning those qualities to them.
- Both hands-gestures: Even when you are holding notes, if your message is appropriately delivered with two hands, use both. To gesture with one hand while the other holds your notes sends a signal of incongruence and woodenness.
- Gestural grace notes: In classical Indian music, as a note fades away, you hear modulations or semitones. These are called grace notes; they add grace and style to the music. In the same manner, when you gesture, get your hand out in front of you, then do something with it. Move it as you emphasize a word, and you will add grace to your presentation.

Nonverbal communication represents a hidden language in presentation work. Because it is linked to the limbic system and not the neocortex, its messages are received outside of consciousness and influence how we feel about a presenter and the presenter's credibility. An enormous amount of information is available today about premier presenting and teaching. Ewing and Grinder's work are just two sources. Another educator, Jon Saphier, has organized the sum of the process-product research on teaching, and more (Saphier and Gower, 1987) and is also continually in classrooms studying good teachers. These three resources alone would fuel an ambitious staff development calendar for a good five years. I've had the good fortune to spend time with both Grinder and Saphier in seminars. I wish that every presenter could, and that we could share this knowledge base with others for the spread of magical teaching and learning in all our classrooms for all our students.

Closings

"This is an excellent workshop, so far," a participant beamed at me during the morning break. You may have heard such comments, while wryly noting the participant's indirect claim to reserve final judgment until the session was completely over, evaluation forms turned in, and people gone home.

At one level I know that the way I close a presentation or workshop will influence participants' final impressions and will be reflected on rating forms. I also know that closings have at least five purposes that are directly related to attaining my instructional goals, and I can combine or select from them to complete a presentation. The proper closing can help participants to (1) sort and store for memory, (2) develop community, (3) continue an inquiry, (4) experience personal growth, and (5) make a commitment. There are also occasions for a closing *before* the end of a presentation, and even as a *first* order of business.

Memory

"The mind can hold only what the seat can endure" is an adage that, like many, is partially true but lacks precision. Most information-processing models reveal that our minds are biologically limited to being able to manage only seven bits of information simultaneously (plus or minus two) in our short-term or working memory. But there is no limit to the complexity and number of subparticles of each of those bits. "Sort and store" closings help participants organize information for retention into a few complex chunks that can more easily be accessed and utilized. Examples of this type of closing include asking participants to outline a personal action plan, list key points they plan to tell someone, or write a brief narrative summarizing concepts important for them to remember.

It's often advantageous to use an early-close version of a "sort and store," particularly after the presentation of dense information or as a transition between topics. Suzanne Bailey of Bailey Associates taught me the "three-balloon" early close, in which participants are encouraged to write a word or phrase that is important for them to remember on each of three imaginary balloons. They then each share these with another participant and explain their choices. Another early-close method is for participants to take two minutes of notes that capture information they want to be sure to remember.

Community

When presentation goals move beyond individual knowledge or skills acquisition to include collegiality and teamwork, it may be appropriate for the closing moments to extend a pathway into those feelings and behaviors. In one form of this closing, the presenter invites open-ended comments about "this experience or anyone in the room." The presenter employs extended wait time and simple nods or thank-yous to acknowledge contributions.

Continuing Inquiry

Norman Sprinthall and Lois Thies Sprinthall (1983) report intriguing and disturbing findings about adult development. On tests of cognitive development, ego development, and moral reasoning, adults in fields of work other than teaching demonstrated continuing growth over the course of their careers. Teachers, measured on the same instruments, did not. Why? What organizational culture factors might contribute to this? What might be the implications for staff development?

Imagine this data being delivered at the end of a workshop. When the workshop goal is "opensure," not closure, such provocative and unanswered data at the end of a workshop can invite reflection and inquiry long after the day's evaluation forms have been submitted. It may be particularly useful when the session is part of an ongoing series of seminars designed to promote changes in perception, practices, and policy. Such information-processing closings, reflecting J. Richard Suchman's early work in Inquiry Training, interact with the mind's strong need to resolve dissonance and work on ongoing theory building and problem solving.

Personal Growth

All journeys begin with a simple picture. Any goal, and the steps leading to it, are first represented in one's mind. These representations, which are often unconscious patterns of pictures, feelings, sounds, smells, or tastes, can be coaxed to consciousness and shaped to not only foreshadow growth but to mold attainment. The presenter stimulates and accelerates growth toward personally defined workshop-related goals by inviting participants to envision themselves engaged in future activities in which they successfully employ the new skills they are refining. The following is an example:

> As you think about a presentation you will make in the near future, see yourself experimenting with a closing that you wish to use. You are with a particular group and you've selected a specific goal for the ending. See what you are wearing and how you appear to the group. Now hear the words you say, noticing your tone of voice and rhythms of speech. See the audience's reaction. Notice how you feel. Watch the group in your mind's eye and adjust your closing until you have it just right and are getting the desired response.

In this example of a mental rehearsal of a closing that helps participants experience personal growth, the presenter literally engages the mind in producing the neurological responses necessary for successful task completion. Notice that the language is very broad and nonspecific, allowing the presenter, like a tailor, to provide the fabric and the listeners to construct from it their own garment. Notice, too, that most of the senses are used. The richer and more varied the internal representation (pictures, sounds, feelings, smells), the more complex the neurological activity and the more likely the actual attainment.

In another type of foreshadowing of personal growth, the presenter alerts participants to the probable hazards along the way and makes suggestions for overcoming them. "People at work like you just the way you are and may be uncomfortable with changes you wish to make. You might find it useful to talk to them, saying, 'I'm working on improving these skills. Will you support me?'"

Commitment

Finally, presenters can close in ways that extend and support participants' own commitment to action. Providing structure and time in which to outline the next steps in a plan, formulate objectives, or identify potential barriers to overcome will move participants one step closer to action. Sometimes, in closing a Cognitive Coaching℠ practicum (Sparks, 1990), trainers have participants conduct a planning conference with each other regarding personal plans they have formulated. Talking out loud with a colleague who nonjudgmentally responds in ways that evoke greater clarity, detail, and imagination is an especially powerful aid to action.

From Ken Blanchard, author of *The One-Minute Manager* and other popular leadership literature, I learned a closing that comes at the beginning of a session! Ken notes that the typical Likert scale evaluation form distributed at the end of a presentation is received too late for the presenter to alter her or his behavior. He distributes it first, and asks if anyone objects to the workshop quality being a straight "5," if that is the top of the scale. Hearing no objections, he encourages people to let him know "the moment he is drifting from a 5." In that way, he shares responsibility for presentation success with the learners, an effective strategy in closing the psychological distance between presenter and participants and for increasing adult learning.

End Notes

Allen, S. & Wollman, J. (1987). *How to Be Funny: Discovering the Comic You*. New York: McGraw-Hill.

Berry, S.E. & Garmston, R.J. (1987). Become a state-of-the-art presenter. *Training and Development Journal* 41(1): 19–23.

Costa, A. (1991). Some thoughts on transfer. Unpublished paper. Berkeley, CA: Institute for Intelligent Behavior.

Costa, A. & Garmston, R. (1994). *Cognitive Coaching: A Foundation for Renaissance Schools*. Norwood, MA: Christopher-Gordon Publishers, Inc.

Decialdini, R. (1984). *The New Psychology of Modern Persuasion*. New York: Simon & Schuster.

Dilts, R. (1989). *Pathways to Leadership Seminar Booklet*. Santa Cruz, CA: Dynamic Learning Center.

Elgin, S.H. (1990). *Staying Well With the Gentle Art of Verbal Self-Defense*. Englewood Cliffs, NJ: Prentice Hall.

Ewing, I. (1994). *The Best Presentation Skills*. Singapore: Ewing Communications Pte Ltd.

Garmston, R., & Wellman, B. (1992). *How to Make Presentations That Teach and Transform*. Alexandria, VA: Association for Supervision and Curriculum Development.

Gibb, J.R. (1978). *Trust: A New View of Personal and Organizational Development*. Los Angeles: Guild of Tutors Press.

Grinder, M. (1993). *Envoy: Your Personal Guide to Classroom Management*. Battle Ground, WA: Michael Grinder & Associates.

Lambert, L. (1995). *The Constructivist Leader*. New York: Teachers College Press.

Lipton, L. (1996). *Making Learning Meaningful: Strategic Teaching for Connectedness.* Unpublished manuscript.

Nickerson, S. (1995). Breaking the language barrier. *Training and Development Journal* 49(2): 45–48.

Noonan, P. (1990). *What I Saw at the Revolution: A Political Life in the Reagan Era*. New York: Random House.

Ornstein, R. (1991). *The Evolution of Consciousness*. New York: Prentice Hall.

Perkins, D. & Salomon, G. (1991). Teaching for transfer. In A. Costa (ed.), *Developing Minds: A Resource Book for Teaching Thinking*. Alexandria, VA: Association for Supervision and Curriculum Development.

Rowe, M.B. (1986). Wait time: Slowing down may be a way of speeding up! *Journal of Teacher Education 23:* 43–49.

Saphier, J. & Gower, R. (1987). *The Skillful Teacher: Building Your Teaching Skills.* Carlisle, MA: Research for Better Teaching, Inc.

Sparks, D. (1990). Cognitive coaching: An interview with Robert Garmston. *Journal of Staff Development* 11(2): 12–15.

Sprinthall, N. & Thies-Sprinthall, L. (1983). The teacher as an adult learner: A cognitive development view. In G. Griffin (ed.), *Staff Development: Eighty-second Yearbook of the National Society for the Study of Education*. Part II Chicago: University of Chicago Press.

True, H. (1995). The power of humor. *Speaking Secrets of the Masters*. Harrisburg, PA: Executive Books.

Weiner, A. (1989). *Speak With Impact Seminar*. Sherman Oaks, CA: Communication Development Associates, Inc.

Whitmore, J. (1994). *Coaching for Performance: A Practical Guide for Growing Your Own Skills*. London: Nicholas Brealey Publishing, Ltd.

Wohlmuth, E. (1983). *The Overnight Guide to Public Speaking*. Philadelphia: Running Press.

CHAPTER 4 How to Add Heart and Punch through Stories

> *The storyteller looks down, strokes his chin whiskers, and smiles. "Ahhh," he [says], and, as he scratches again he explains to you that in the course of his own wanderings he has discovered that when he tells his tales, those who listen actually* live those adventures *inside of themselves. In fact, he continues (and here he looks up at you with mischievous eyes), in fact, people are living amazing adventures all the time.*
>
> David Gordon

Can you remember a time when you've been deeply touched by a speech or presentation? It's very likely that what made that experience so moving for you was not the data or ideas, but the stories that carried those thoughts to your heart.

You tell stories already, even if you are not conscious of making them a regular part of your presentation repertoire. The purpose of this chapter is to offer a range of ideas with which you can extend your storytelling voice, and add heart and punch to your presentations. I can clearly remember the time when I first gave myself permission to tell stories to groups. I was completing a seminar with John Grinder, a master at weaving metaphors through his teaching. At that time I was as terrified of storytelling as some people are of public speaking. I was afraid that it wasn't a good use of the audience's time, that it would take away from the important concepts that could be communicated. With Grinder's modeling and encouragement, I decided to try. I found my fears had been dead wrong. The moment I began to tell stories, my own and those I had heard from others, I started to have more fun. So did my audiences. And, I suspect, they carried away more in their hearts and their minds.

Finding the Story

Notes from a Safari Journal

We had two treats at lunch time today. We stopped at a dry riverbed near Olduvai Gorge. Acacia and aloe plants provided shade. Sue spotted a leopard turtle near where the stream runs in the rainy season. We scampered down to photograph it. We returned to the Land Rover, where Juma waited, and began to eat our sandwiches. Suddenly and silently, a small figure appeared. I guessed him to be about ten years old, a young Masai shepherd on a break from his duties. Shyly he stood nearby. He spoke no Swahili, and Juma spoke no Masai, so we all conversed as well as we could with gestures and a few sounds. A scraggly brown dog was his companion. He held his spear comfortably, as if he had been born with it, along with his ebony skin and contrasting white necklace. We shared some food with him. When he left, Juma told us a story. "It was right here," he started, "that I saw for the first time the migration of the wildebeest. . . ."

"Write them down" is the first tip I've learned from experienced speakers and storytellers when I've asked how to find stories. Often our best yarns come from personal experiences or an anecdote someone has told us in an informal conversation. When your radar is keen for story content, you'll collect these for later development. Of course, there are many sources of stories beyond your own biography. Figure 4.1 identifies some sources for presentation stories. The best story sources start with you.

Personal Stories

The *autobiographical story* is special because it is truly yours. It's very personal and shares something about yourself with the audience, with whatever point you are using it to illustrate. The safari theme throughout this book is an example of using an autobiographical source to create a "wraparound" story. At the time I was on safari, I certainly had no idea that I would use my experiences in Africa to support a book about presentation skills. What I did know was that the experience was special to me and that I wanted to remember it. And so I wrote it down. Each day—well, most days—I spent time with my journal, recording things

- Personal
  - Autobiographical
  - Signature
- Biographical
- History, Literature, and the Arts
- Indirect
  - Allegory
  - Metaphor
- Culturally Held
  - Your Culture
  - Other Cultures
  - Organizational Culture
- Case Study
- Demonstrations

Figure 4.1: Finding the Story

I'd seen, names of plants and animals and birds I had learned from Juma, and impressions from the day.

(By the way, our guide's name was John, not Juma. But as a storyteller I needed a name that would convey that he was African, not a European poaching off this beautiful continent. I needed a name that suggested he was of the land, intimately knowledgeable about the rhythms and patterns of life in Africa. He was all of that and more. The stories about Africa that I've included in this book have been real. Only the guide's name has been changed. And so a certain liberty is granted in crafting a personal story to produce the desired effect.)

So, write everything down. Details help audiences form pictures in their minds. Without writing them down, I can neither remember the details nor fully reexperience the events for my own pleasure.

The sources for personal stories are all aspects of your life. Your early childhood, adolescent years, and experiences as a student can be particularly poignant, because they help audiences connect with the child in all of us. Your family, recreational pursuits, and times of adversity are great corners into which to peek for story content. When telling a story of personal adversity, punch it up by telling the group what you learned from it.

A *signature story* is about something that is autobiographically you, that contributes to your uniqueness, and that illustrates a theme in your life. Signature stories can be told many times to many different audiences. If you have ever heard the poet Maya Angelou speak, you've probably heard her tell about her childhood and being raised by a relative of hers in the South. If you are like me, you've probably not thought of your life as having a signature story. You may be surprised if you take a look. For example, something occurred to me while I was writing this book that led me to reveal the following story. It could be a vignette from my own signature story.

> Have you ever felt really left out—like other people were special, but not you? Well, I was born out of wedlock and adopted at birth. My adopted mom died within my first year. I was a student in classes for children with behavior problems (before there were special education classes), and I spent more than a third of my childhood in children's homes. At Lytton Home, set on sprawling acres filled with oak trees (four "cottages" to house the boys and a main building for the girls), I grew very close to my social worker, Marabel, and her husband. Bob ran a dairy farm that adjoined the property of the children's home. It was there that I experienced my first bonding with an adult male, someone who modeled for me what it meant to be a man. Several kids from the home used to work on the farm for Bob. During my late teens, they adopted one of the kids at the home, Tom Moore. We called him Gabby. In his early twenties he drove off a bridge and was killed. A few years later, they adopted another boy from the home. Both of these boys were buddies of mine. We had pitched hay, milked cows, and shoveled you-know-what together. The second kid to be adopted was Duncan McLeod. A few years later he died in a drowning accident. At the time of both adoptions, I had conflicting feelings. I was happy for Gabby and Mac, but at some level I wondered, "Why not me?" At some level, that vague feeling of being outside the fold existed throughout the rest of my life.
>
> Then something quite incredible happened right after my sixtieth birthday. My wife and I stopped in San Diego to visit King and Alice Hart, a couple who had taken me in as a foster child during my sixteenth year and with whom I had maintained close contact ever since. Over dinner they announced that it now seemed possible that I was going to "turn out okay" and perhaps it was time to make the relationship legal. Would it be all right with me if they were to become my adopted parents? My heart grew to twice its size, and I answered yes.
>
> We appeared before a judge in juvenile court to sign papers. We checked in, passed through a metal detector, and had our possessions searched by a uniformed policeman. I was a sixty-year-old child, and my adopting parents were in their mid-eighties. The judge was the youngest person present. The brief ceremony was completed, and my dream of being adopted by someone I cared for was realized.

> What I learned from that experience was the magical nature of symbols and ceremony. I've been, for whatever reason, adverse to them all my life. Yet that gesture on their part, for it is truly a gesture—there is no rich estate, heirlooms, or debts to inherit—has modified most of my waking hours since the event. I feel loved unconditionally, as a child feels loved by a parent. I feel fully well, and I realize that for most of my life I've lived as if I've been slightly under the weather. Yet what has changed? Nothing. Their love for me has been constant, as has mine for them. Yet everything has changed. I know, with my heart, my metaphorical mind, and the deepest fiber of my being, that I am loved and that I belong.
>
> I also learned that it is never too late to say you love someone.

My sense is that signature stories need to be handled rather carefully. Their purpose is not to adorn oneself with mystique or sympathy but to illustrate a specific point. To accomplish this probably requires a certain level of detachment, as if you are reporting events, not reliving them. I think, too, that the signature story is probably more appropriate for keynote speeches than for more intimate presentations to smaller groups.

Biographical Stories

Another great source for story content is the lives of people about whom you have read: the greats and the near greats, political figures, artists, athletes, movie stars, scientists, civil rights workers, and spiritual leaders. Although many famous historical anecdotes are probably apocryphal (which means that they may never have happened), they are too good not to use. Here are some examples:

> Whenever Ben Franklin was confronted with a difficult decision, he would take a sheet of paper and draw a line down the middle of it. On one side he wrote, "Reasons For" and on the other, "Reasons Against."
>
> Abraham Lincoln used to argue both sides of the case when he was presenting to a jury. He would take the opposition's side, then he would take his client's side. He was very careful to bring out more points in his own favor, but when he took the opposition's side he was always fair, although he was undoubtedly not quite as eloquent as when he presented his client's case.

Use this type of story when you wish to persuade listeners that a certain behavior has merit because it was a practice of someone important.

History, Literature, and the Arts

In Irving Stone's *Men to Match My Mountains* (1956), a compelling history of California, Nevada, Colorado, and Arizona from the 1840s to the 1880s is told through stories. The book is a wonderful glimpse into circumstances of bravery, vision, perseverance, economics, politics, creativity, and just plain dumb luck. I discovered this book when I was teaching fifth grade and told stories to my students endlessly in connection with our study of the western movement in U.S. history. (It's interesting that I could tell stories to students then, but not to adults.)

The possibilities for stories from this category are endless. Remember to consider telling stories from motion pictures or what appears on television. The old *I Love Lucy* show has many zany vignettes to illustrate styles of managing conflict; the movie *Courage under Fire* illustrates the various perspectives from which different persons may remember the same event; and the film treatment of novelist John Grishman's *A Time to Kill* reveals the pervasiveness and complexity of prejudice. *Seinfeld* uses many wonderfully comic illustrations with which one could teach paraphrasing. Later in this chapter, I'll show how an episode from *The Mary Tyler Moore Show* might be used.

Indirect Stories

Much has been learned about how to craft indirect stories for the unconscious mind. Before exploring some of these ideas, two definitions will be useful: allegory and metaphor. From my reading of Webster's dictionary, *allegory* seems to relate more to story form, whereas *metaphor* is used to describe a certain use of a word or phrase. Yet the bulk of the literature on storytelling refers to the indirect or figurative tale as metaphor. Because of this common usage, I have used the term *metaphor* in the sections that follow to describe the structure of stories designed for the unconscious mind.

Allegory (from the Greek): a description of one thing under the image of another; from *allos*, "other," and *agoreuein*, "to speak in the assembly"; a story in which people, things, and events have another meaning, as in a fable or parable. Allegories are used for teaching or explaining.

The *Dictionary of Word Origins* treats this word in a more memorable fashion. It defines *allegory* as "one story with another hidden inside." From *allos*, "other," and *agoria*, "speech" (Shipley, 1959).

Metaphor (from the Greek): a transferring to one word the sense of another. From *metapherein: meta*, "over," and *pherein*, "to bear"; a figure of speech in which one thing is likened to another different thing by being spoken of as it were that other: an implied comparison, in which a word or phrase that is ordinarily and primarily used of one thing is applied to another (e.g., "screaming headlines," "all the world's a stage"). Roger Jones, the author of *Physics As Metaphor* (1982), defines metaphor as "an evocation of the inner connection among things."

Later I will describe the physiological response to indirect stories and the linguistic structures that allow them to communicate effectively beyond our conscious attention.

Here are two tips for the presenter who is using indirect stories. In Chapter 1, four audience types were described. While indirect stories or metaphors are appropriate for each of them, the audience types that appreciate them best are the "friends" and the "scientists." Simple metaphors work well with the "professors," but extended stories of this nature may be met with some impatience by this data-driven group. Also, when developing your own indirect story, look for ideas in the natural universe: seasons, growing things, animal life, weather, and the solar system. The new sciences—chaos theory, quantum physics, complexity theory, fractal mathematics—are excellent sources. The natural world provides vigorously authentic themes for stories because they are recognized as true in the precognitive parts of our being.

Culturally Held Stories

The tales in this group may be allegorical, may record a historical event, or may be in the nature of a fable. They are well known by the dominant culture in which you are presenting. For most of us this is the dominant culture of the United States. The goose that laid the golden egg, Paul Bunyan and his blue ox, George Washington chopping down the cherry tree, Martin Luther King's "I Have a Dream" speech. Ernest Hemingway's *The Old Man and the Sea* or *The Pearl,* the stories in *Grimms' Fairy Tales,* and biblical tales like the prodigal son are examples of this type of story. Since they are well known, they serve as a common reference point in bringing home a point.

Another kind of culturally held story is one that, like a popular song, seems to have an ongoing life span. These often make a point through tapping into our emotions. The person who throws a starfish into the sea on a beach where hundreds lie stranded, saying, "Well, I made a difference for that one," is an example of this type of story. Many of these can be found in books like *Chicken Soup for the Soul* by Jack Canfield and Mark Hansen (1993).

You can also tell stories from a completely different cultural tradition than the audience's. As long as you can explain the context and it is relevant, people will enjoy hearing this class of story. In fact, when selecting stories for indirect communication, these have an advantage. Because they require more effort from the conscious mind to follow the story line, the less direct messages can more freely interact with the unconscious. I'll say more later on the theory of how that works. From this continent, Native American stories tap rich ways of knowing; from the Middle East, Sufi stories draw from Muslim wisdom; from Asia, Zen and Buddhist themes are useful. For mythology from around the world, Joseph Campbell is the best source. His *Historical Atlas of World Mythology* (1988) is scholarly, illustrated, and a delightful series. Campbell urges us to find ourselves in the stories of other cultures and even from primitive mythology. In *Primitive Mythology* (1987), he says:

> The comparative study of the mythologies of the world compels us to view the cultural history of mankind as a unit; for we find that such themes as the fire-theft, deluge, land of the dead, virgin birth, and resurrected hero have a worldwide distribution—appearing everywhere in new combinations while remaining, like the elements of a kaleidoscope, only a few and always the same.

A final type of cultural story is one that lives in the work culture of a particular organization. These stories have two goals: one is to symbolize the overarching goals and values of the group; the other is to provide suggestions, through story, about how participants should act. Four characteristics set these stories apart from other types of culturally held stories.

1. *They are real.* They are told about real people, describe specific actions, convey a specific set of time and place, and are connected with the values of the organization.
2. *They are known.* People in the organization not only know the story, they know that others know it and act in accordance with its guidance.
3. *They are believed.* The point the story makes is believed to be true of the organization.
4. *They model social contracts.* The story describes how things are to be done or not done and describes associated rewards and punishments.

These stories are often about equality versus inequality, security versus insecurity, or independence versus interdependence. Popular management books, like *A Passion for Excellence* by Tom Peters and Nancy Austin (1985) and *Management by Storying Around: A New Method of Leadership* by David Armstrong (1992), are usually filled with these types of stories. Here is an example from A *Passion for Excellence*:

> Once you realize the importance of stories, you can begin to think of yourself, in part, as a story-trail creator. Domino's Pizza Distribution: Don Vicek recalls the speed and impact with which a certain story traveled through his system. He was visiting a distribution center. He noticed some unacceptably lumpy dough. As he tells it, "The quality wasn't right. We couldn't let it go out. I stopped, I rolled up my sleeves, and I worked with the local team to fix the procedure. In twenty-four hours, the news had traveled twenty-five hundred miles! I got a call from one of my centers on the other side of the continent: 'Don, we heard about what you did. That's great. That's the kind of commitment to quality we need. We're behind you out here. We'll redouble our efforts.' You had to have been there to believe it."

Real stories—appropriate for your school, of course—come from real events in your setting. I once tried to start such a story in a district by encouraging a person, who was in charge of a three-day summer workshop for school-site councils, to send all the councils home if their principal was not with them. I did this because the importance of principal participation in such endeavors is invaluable and irreplaceable. I also knew that such a "story" would reverberate for years in the culture of the workplace and send an intentional message about expectations for principal leadership.

Case Study

A final type of verbal story on which I'll comment is the case study. In many ways this is like a story or an anecdote, the most obvious difference being that you can't change the facts when telling it. Case studies are useful for explaining theoretical concepts or for advocating a certain approach to working with a situation. Here are three tips on delivering this type of story: (1) always cite your source; (2) construct the story line so that it is provocative, raising a question in the listeners' minds; and (3) remember that your choice of this story type is for propaganda. (You could have selected other examples, you know.) Be open to the audience's being disturbed and/or challenging the studies you cite.

Demonstrations

It is very true that a picture is worth a thousand words. Steve McQueen is reported to have advised another actor to always say the last word in a scene, and never say anything that you can act out. If you can do it, don't say it. Give audiences the option of switching modalities to follow your message. It helps to keep the brain, and learning, stimulated. See the section on copresenting later in this chapter for some special ways of demonstrating this with a partner.

It is said that Michelangelo, in setting out to carve a piece of marble, would visit it when it was penetrated by the first rays of sunlight so he might discover the figure hidden inside. He describes much of his sculpting as releasing the sculpture inside the stone. In just such a way, you will find the stories that work best for you, in the categories above and in the suggestions that follow.

Tell Me a Story

Stories are important. They keep us alive. In the ships, in the camps, in the quarters, fields, prisons, on the road, on the run, underground, under siege, in the throes, on the verge—the storyteller snatches us back from the edge to hear the next chapter, in which we are the subjects.

Toni Cae Bambara, *Salvation Is the Issue*

I sit on the floor, my back leaning against a file cabinet, piles of books on the dark carpet around me. I open another book and squint through the index for entries like storytelling, stories, or metaphor. My index finger browses through the table of contents. Nothing. Now I have examined most of the books in my modest collection on presentation skills and speech making. Three are left on the bottom shelf of the bookcase. Again, fruitlessly I search their pages.

Well-told stories are the signature of the accomplished presenter. Why is it that books on presenting do not address this important art? Perhaps it is because, as I discovered in writing this chapter, storytelling is not easy to write about briefly. It is, however, complex enough that entire books are devoted to the subject. I'll mention two excellent ones later. Since my own presentations have improved so much since I've added stories, I decided to try to share here, briefly, a few helpful ideas.

Why Tell Stories?

Why are stories such useful presentation tools? I suggest three reasons: (1) they personalize presentation content, sending forth a gossamer filament that connects the audience and the presenter; (2) they open windows to the intuitive knowledge of an audience; and (3) they can tap the resources of the unconscious mind.

Facts, data, theories, and statistics contribute richly to learning but can uniformly be read in any book, heard on any audiotape, and seen on any screen. Stories, however, extend facts to knowing and presenting the topic in a *personal* way, in part because the presenter's nonverbal behavior changes when telling a story. Voice pattern, tone, inflection, facial animation, gestures, and use of floor space shift. The audience sees, hears, and feels more of who you are through the very act of telling a story.

Stories also tap the wells of intuitive knowledge. We *know* in at least three ways: (1) rationally, aided by our logical and often linear thinking processes; (2) empirically, by what we feel and see and hear; and (3) metaphorically. To know something metaphorically is to understand it intuitively. Stories open us up to the symbolic dimensions of experience and to the multiple meanings that may coexist, each giving extra shades of meaning to the other.

Finally, a certain type of story can engage our unconscious minds in ways that bring resolution to problems, shift us from distressed emotional states to more positive ones, and offer resources for self-healing. Such stories have existed for thousands of years in many cultures. It is only recently that psychologists and linguists have identified what it is about certain stories that engages the unconscious. These stories speak first to the right hemisphere of the brain, activating images and emotions that are then communicated in word symbols to the slightly more ponderous left hemisphere of the brain. Later in this chapter I'll describe the linguistic and physiological mechanisms for this. Here, I'll mention two remarkable books that describe the process:

David Gordon's *Therapeutic Metaphors* (1978) and Joyce Mills and Richard Crowley's *Therapeutic Metaphors for Children and the Child Within* (1986).

Tips for Telling Stories

I once watched a nationally known presenter answer audience members' questions. It struck me as unusual that he balanced on one foot while he listened to the questions, much like a stork or a person poised to move in any direction. I remember thinking at the time how that might be a manifestation of a certain fluidity or flexibility within him. Telling stories calls on the same inner resources. Here are some tips you may find useful to build, expand, and fine-tune your own storytelling repertoire.

- First, plan new presentations without regard to stories. Once your objectives are clear and your content and sequence have been decided, ask yourself the question, "What story do I know that could support this presentation?"
- Choose, when you can, personal-experience stories related to home, family, recreation, childhood, or work. Hone them for audience consumption by rehearsing them once or twice. Such stories are valuable because you "know" them deeply. Be careful to tell personal stores, not private ones. Reserve private stories for close friends. Audiences can become uncomfortable when you share information that's too private. "I'm an alcoholic" or "I committed my son to an insane asylum this weekend" doesn't create rapport—it develops discomfort and distance.
- As noted earlier, be alert to story material from books, movies, and television that you can retell and relate to your topic. Use the story types described earlier to help you in your search.
- Start a filing system to collect stories under topics or themes important in your work.
- Plan on-and-off ramps for your stories. These transitions are as important as the stories themselves and must connect the story to the content and the audience to your purpose in telling the story. For example, I sometimes tell a story about a handyman that I met at the end of a trip. I will usually transition into this story by making a remark about the trip that brought me here to this audience, and then say how that reminds me of a time when I met this handyman.
- Select stories that have strong, capable, active, intelligent people in them. This is particularly important when a

woman or a member of an ethnic minority is the main character, because such stories counterbalance the unconscious racism and sexism around us.

- Adapt and give credit for stories that you learn from others. Change the genders, settings, and time periods to suit your objectives. Always give appropriate credit. If you've learned a first person story from another presenter, never claim it as your own. Say, "Here's a story person X tells."
- Tell stories to illustrate concepts. Illustrative stories help audiences form a picture of important concepts. For example, I sometimes tell a story about a kindergarten teacher who was attempting to develop trust with another teacher on her staff. As I describe what Peg said and did and how the other teacher responded, participants run a mental movie that imprints for them what occurred and how each reacted. They are treated to an experience that is so graphic that they know clearly what to do in their own relationships and what mistakes not to repeat.

Such teaching stories are used to impart conceptual information. Some of these are indirect and take the form of analogy or metaphor. I will always remember a statement attributed to Madeline Hunter in which she likened the mind to wet cement. The first idea to get there sticks. If the information is incorrect, you may have to trowel it out a hundred times to dislodge it. The image she offered has stuck with me for years.

While all stories modify brain activity and energy flow, some stories create special mental shifts to keep participants alert, resourceful, and capable of receiving more information. Humorous stories, jokes, and one-liners are especially helpful.

Finally, some stories invite reflection. Usually these are of a serious nature, paint pictures of accomplishment, frustration, joy, or dismay and touch people emotionally. In another form of reflection, dissonance is created, and questions are raised but not answered. Reflective stories are crafted for the unconscious mind and draw on the principles described in the two books mentioned earlier. Next, let's examine the metaphor as a gentle alchemist in mental transformation.

What's a Meta Phor?

Imagine a group of adults listening to a story—the entire audience rocking in the same rhythm at the same time. This scene actually happened at a recent storytelling festival. Storyteller Nell

Shivers of Raymond, Mississippi and an audience, comfortably seated in rocking chairs that just happened to be on display by a fellow artisan, were caught on tape by a television reporter.

What was happening—a deep relaxation, an entrainment, a light trance, or a focused state of inner consciousness? Literally, all of the above were happening. Carter-Liggett, at the Pacific Graduate School of Psychology in Palo Alto, California, theorizes that during a story, listeners experience a biochemical change that involves a decrease in the hormone cortisol and an increase in the concentration of immunoglobulin A. This change shows up in the listners' saliva and is related to the story's capacity to relax them and engage the right hemisphere of the brain, which is the wellspring not only of imagery but of our capacity to deal with change as well. Carter-Liggett hopes to have the research to prove this in the future.

But that's not all. Brain research is also revealing more about how our minds process metaphor. A simplified version of some of these findings are:

- the left brain hemisphere processes language sequentially, logically, and literally;
- the right brain hemisphere processes in simultaneous, holistic, and implicative fashion.

In one study, medical students who were reading and writing technical passages registered the highest left hemispheric activity, whereas the highest right hemispheric activity was recorded when reading Sufi stories. The Sufi stories produced the same left hemispheric activity as the technical matter *plus* a surge of involvement in the right hemisphere (Mills and Crowley 1986).

Some languages require higher right-brain activity than others. In Hopi, for example, words do not have fixed meanings but are understood only in relation to the entire communication. A story delivered in Hopi requires greater contextual understanding, and hence more right-hemisphere engagement, than the same story in English. Japanese, too, lives in the right brain.

Since metaphor depends on implication more than on literal meaning, it would seem likely that more right-brain activity would be needed to decode its meaning than would be needed for analytical, logical communications.

Metaphor Is the Mind's Way of Knowing

Other understandings of how metaphor interacts with the mind are offered by psychologists and linguists. Psychologists like Carl

Jung, Julian James, Milton Erickson, and Ernest Rossi believe that metaphor *is* the process of the subjective, unconscious mind. Linguists John Grinder and Richard Bandler conclude that metaphor operates on a kind of triadic principle, in which its meaning moves through three different stages. Their work is based on traditional linguistic studies and on their own documentation of the work of Milton Erickson, a therapist and hypnotist who used story extensively to communicate with the unconscious mind. (Erickson's view is that if the conscious mind could have solved the problem a person brought to him, it would have already done so.) The three stages are as follows:

1. The meaning of the story is literal. This is called the *surface structure* of the story.
2. The meaning of the story is associated with some generic or impersonal thoughts or data. The listener may reflect on the tragedy of war, for example, or ponder the sadness of relationships breaking up, or remember a movie in which the same theme was present.
3. The meaning of the story is recovered from deep within the listener's personal experience. The listener may remember feeling sad at the death of a parent or feeling loss from a marriage breakup. This is the level at which the metaphor has its greatest potency. Sometimes these recovered meanings are below the level of a person's consciousness.

"Once the personal connection occurs ... an interactive loop is established between the story and the listener's inner world by which the story is enlivened and further extended" (Mills and Crowley, 1986). This process is referred to as a *transderivational search*.

Of course, not all storytelling produces such visible effects. The anecdote, the one-liner, and the joke may evoke interest but not deeper processing. Stories that engage the mind in making translations from a literal mental language to the analogic, from word thinking to picture thinking, and from left brain to right brain—in other words, metaphors—may indeed produce these biochemical, hemispheric, and meaning-making shifts. Speakers and staff developers who are working to employ more metaphor in their work frequently do so for at least four reasons.

Four Purposes of Metaphor

Metaphors are not always verbal but can be physical expressions of an idea, such as dance or body sculpting. They can also be concrete, such as shaking a penny inside an inflated balloon—

1. Surface Structure. Literal meaning: the words carry what the literal story elements mean—pictures, characters, settings, actions, etc.
2. Deep Structure. Associated meaning: the words are associated with (stimulate) thoughts or information of a general or impersonal nature.
3. Deeper Structure. Recovered meaning: the words stimulate recall of a personal connection, experience, feeling, or conclusion.
4. Once the personal connection has been made, an interactive loop is established between the story and the listener's inner world. The meaning (often unconscious) of the story is further enlivened and extended.

Figure 4.2: Transderivational Search

symbolizing the trial and error required to get change going, and how, once in motion, it takes on a life of its own. Metaphors can also be visual, as in cartoons or movies, or they can appear in organizing systems, such as murals or ceremonies (Bailey, 1993).

Teachers and staff developers use metaphor on at least four occasions: (1) to teach new concepts, (2) to create and generate new ideas, (3) to empower or capacitate others, and (4) to guide groups in change processes. I will comment on each of these here and then describe more extensively five specific ways of using metaphor to empower and support change.

- **Teach New Concepts**

  Metaphoric aids are useful when the presenter wishes to teach content that is new to the learners and wants to build on their understanding of another system and transfer it to the new topic. Teachers use metaphor when they introduce a new concept by relating it to something they presume to be in the students' experience. An old Chinese story makes this point well.

  Someone complained to the prince that Hui Zi was always using parables. "Please forbid him, so that his meanings will be clear," the prince was asked.

  The prince met with Hui Zi "From now on," he said, "kindly talk in a straightforward manner and not in parables."

"Suppose there was a man who did not know what a catapult is," replied Hui Zi. "If he asked you what it looked like, and you told him it looked just like a catapult, would he understand what you mean?"

"Of course not," answered the prince.

"But suppose you told him that a catapult looks something like a bow and that it is made of bamboo—wouldn't he understand you better?"

"Yes, that would be clearer," admitted the prince.

"We compare something a man does not know with something he does know in order to help him to understand it," said Hui Zi. "If you won't let me use parables, how can I make things clear to you?" (Mills and Crowley, 1986).

To teach the meaning of "Dolby stereo," for example, one might say, "Dolby is like a sonic laundry. It washes the dirt (the noise) out of the clothes (the signal) without disturbing the clothes (the signal)" (Von Oech, 1983). Technically, from a linguistic perspective, the phrase *is like* makes this a simile. But according to Charles Faulkner (1991), the mind doesn't make this distinction.

- **Generate Ideas**

  Synectic exercises, in which participants are asked to list the ways in which one item is like another, are well-known devices for creating lots of new ideas about a topic. Bruce Wellman often gives groups 4 x 6 cards on which he has pasted a variety of images clipped from magazines. He asks each group to pick one picture and decide in what ways this item is like the topic they have been studying.

- **Empower Others**

  Stories can help people access the emotional and cognitive resources they need when they are overwhelmed with

negative feelings, trapped in egocentric or ethnocentric states, fixated in the past, or operating within a view of reality that limits choices. Stories that open up choices, present overarching perspectives, illuminate potential solutions, or build common ground assist people in getting in touch with the internal resources they need to resolve their own difficulties.

- **Guide Groups in Change Processes**

  Suzanne Bailey is a master of this incredibly potent use of metaphors. Here is an example of a strategy she has pioneered: Invite change agents to identify themselves with an object, animal, or song of their choosing, related to a specific situation or group. Now ask them to imagine an object, animal, or song they would be for maximum effectiveness. Finally, have them think about the ways in which they would need to change the original metaphor to create the second one. Not long ago, a person in a workshop that Suzanne and I were conducting reported that she saw herself as a Tupperware container and believed she needed to be a net. What must she do to transform the Tupperware? Removing the lid and poking holes in it is a good start, but it may be insufficient. Soon she may find herself looking around for threads of this and that, tying them together, and making a strong but permeable tool. Another person reported that she was a tiger and needed to be a sheep dog. The transition activities for her might be to remove her claws, shorten her fangs, ruffle her hair, and maintain her ferocious and protective capacities, but add the sheep dog's repertoire of friendliness.

When "Try, Try Again" Is Fool's Advice

Much of our efforts at school reform are coldly analytical. We strategize, analyze, categorize. We weigh weaknesses and strengths, opportunities and threats. We list, rank, measure, disaggregate, and assess. We "TQM" (total quality manage) and otherwise alphabetize our students, programs, and improvement efforts. All these efforts are laudable, the tools are useful, and the intentions are good. But if they are used alone, without heart, we'll get what we've always gotten: improvements at a pace and a scale far too slow and far too low to serve the urgent needs of today's children preparing for tomorrow's world.

To elevate metaphorical thought to a level that is equal with analytical thought brings heart to the work. Try as we may, left-brain work does not create art. Yet neither is right-brain work alone sufficient. The power of utilizing the two-sided brain is dramatically demonstrated in accounts of creative discoveries. A good deal of both is usually required.

Stories for the Unconscious Mind

The woodcutter raises the ax. Light glints off the sharply honed edge. As it arcs slowly over the woodcutter's head, whispers of labored breathing and smells of dark fear mingle in the chill day ...

Inside the room, thirty faces fix intently on the speaker. They sit, bodies expectant, breathing slowly as pond water, their faces like photographs of themselves as young children. They are waiting, imagining the next development of the speaker's story, open to new discovery.

What is it about storytelling that makes it such a potent teaching device? The best presenters intuitively know that a *clear story purpose* is the first principle in telling stories that empower others, teach new concepts, generate ideas, or guide groups in change processes. The second principle is *developing a personalized storytelling style*. If, like me, you are still building your tale-telling repertoire with conscious attention to what makes a story work, and you would like to incorporate stories for the unconscious mind, read on.

Which Way Will the Ax Fall? Five Story Purposes

When your purpose is to empower or support people through the personal journey of change, these five specific uses of metaphor are helpful.

1. *Seeding Ideas*: These vignettes and metaphors are sometimes told at the beginning of a session, as part of an "anticipatory set," or during the presentation, to aid participants in considering a topic from a fresh perspective.
2. *Pacing and Leading*: These stories are told to acknowledge and validate existing emotional states and/or points of view, in order to lead to states in which participants are capable of making new choices.
3. *Shining Information through Defensive Structures*: These stories deliver information past defensive filters that are normally capable of blocking the acquisition, and therefore

the potential influence, of new data. This is like allowing the sunlight to filter through spaces created by the irregular placement of timber in a log cabin.

4. *Altering Attitudes or Behavior*: When the workshop behavior of participants is likely to interfere with learning, these stories can influence the necessary behavioral and attitudinal changes.
5. *Setting and Firing Anchors*: These stories establish and use signals capable of evoking a memory, an attitude, or an emotional experience during the presentation.

Following are some examples and considerations in designing or selecting stories for these five purposes.

Stories to Seed Ideas

Consider the transderivational searches (Figure 4.2) that audience members might have made when I opened a full-day problem-solving session with them recently. The presenting problem was that many teachers were angry with the principal. Morale was so bad that the board ordered the principal removed unless she could "turn the school around" by June. I had been called in February to gather data, consult, and help if I could. A partner and I interviewed every staff member—certified and classified—in thirty-minute private conversations. We asked, "What are you feeling good about here? What problems are at this school? What recommendations do you have?" We were shocked to learn that, whereas many teachers were complaining about the principal, many more were complaining about each other. One teacher summarized it as, "We're shooting at our wingmen." The purpose of the day's session was to report the data from the interviews and facilitate the group in a problem-solving conversation. I began with this story.

> Last night I was talking with a gardener. I asked her how she knew when to repot a plant. "When it shows signs of lifelessness." she replied.
>
> "What are some of those signs?" I asked? She explained that the leaves turn brown or brittle and that the roots may force their way out of the bottom of the pot. "So what do you do?" I asked?
>
> "Well, first I break the pot," she said.
>
> "Break it? That sounds so violent. Why do you do that?"
>
> "Well, consider the options," she said. "If I tried to pull the plant out of the pot it had grown too large for, it might go into shock. But if I break the pot, then I can gently and lovingly remove the plant from its shattered pot and place it in a larger one, where there will be enough soil and nutrients for it to grow."

I stared silently at the audience for a long, discomforting moment. Then I said, "Our purpose here today is to ..."

I told this story to seed ideas and prepare this group emotionally. The day was going to be rough; something might be broken, but if so, it would be with loving intent. So hang in there, no matter how uncomfortable it gets. This plant can find new life.

Now, here's another opening in which a story is used to seed for a different class of ideas.

> How do you measure success? For example, consider a man who failed in business at age thirty-one. The following year he was defeated in an election. Then, at age thirty-four, he failed again in business. At thirty-five he overcame the death of his sweetheart. When he was thirty-six, he had a nervous breakdown. Two years later, he lost another election. He lost still another election at age forty-three; three years later he lost another election, and, again, at age forty-eight, he lost yet another election. Each of these lost elections was for a congressional seat. When he was fifty-six, he failed in an effort to become vice president of the United States.
>
> Today we're going to examine how you can determine whether a person is succeeding or failing. Do you focus on life events or on what the person is learning from these events? As we examine the difference between these, we're going to relate them to your own experiences.
>
> The man I've been talking about finally won an election, an important one. He was elected United States president at age sixty. His name was Abraham Lincoln.

Presenters use opening stories to seed ideas at the beginning of workshops or when introducing new topics, as in the examples above. Sometimes presenters tell stories to plant an idea on the opening day of a workshop and reference the growing thought several times later in their work with the group.

An elegant opening for a presentation can focus, energize, and accelerate the development of presenter-audience rapport. Stories like the Lincoln opening are intended to create anticipation and curiosity for what may come. Curiosity can be a traveling companion. The Lincoln introduction, for example, begins to raise dissonance in the listener's mind. This can be the tease that invites fresh concepts.

Stories that carry knowledge from the mute right brain to the left brain—so it can be recognized as being like something that is already known—and do it with laughter are doubly valuable. These stories not only focus participants but also provide the lightness and humor that are valuable to good learning states. Consider the following story, which is sometimes told in Cognitive

Coaching[sm] workshops as a preface to teaching participants the specific strategies for working with not-yet-autonomous persons.

> Remember *The Mary Tyler Moore Show*? On one segment, Ted Baxter was going to get married, and he kept pestering Lou Grant for a man-to-man talk, hoping that Lou would share with him his wisdom and experience in relationships. Lou successfully avoided this awkward conversation with Ted until finally, Ted corners him at a party at Mary's house. "Lou," Ted says, "we've got a few minutes now. Why don't you give me that man-to-man talk I've been wanting, you know, kind of give me some tips that will help me?" Lou, looking exasperated, says, "Okay, Ted. You know the way you do things now?" "Yes," says Ted. "Well," Lou pontificates, "don't do them that way anymore."

"Today," a Cognitive Coaching[sm] trainer might say after that introduction, "we're going to offer you some more specific tools than that for helping people improve."

One reason humor is important is that it helps eliminate the psychological gap between the speaker and audience. The more important a figure, the bigger the gap. John F. Kennedy had the knack for humor. Richard Nixon did not, nor did Jimmy Carter, who once stood up at a dinner for White House correspondents and announced, "I'm not going to say anything of significance, so you can all put away your crayons." The reaction from the roomful of journalists was straight-faced. Given the normally strained relations between the president and the press, the joke went over like a brick (Buck, 1986).

Stories to Pace and Lead

> "Have you ever felt so tired you just wanted to go home and have a cup or tea or space out in front of the TV? One night last week I was on the freeway after work. The traffic was annoying and I was bone tired. I kept thinking, why was I going to a meeting instead of heading home, where I really wanted to be? I wondered what possessed me to sign up for the event, and I realized I had lots of things I'd rather be doing.
>
> As I sat down in the auditorium I looked around at the other people there and wondered who they were, why they were here. And then I watched the speaker begin. I was thinking that I had traded a nice evening at home for this, and he'd better be worth it. As I settled in my seat and listened, I began to be curious, and, after a while I noticed I was getting interested. Before I knew it, I realized I was pleased that I'd come because I was getting practical ideas that I could use the very next day.

The foregoing account of feelings preceding and beginning a meeting is fairly common. Speakers frequently pace a group's subjective experience as a prerequisite to leading them toward an emotional state that is desirable for the context and purpose of the presentation. To *pace* means to honor an existing state and make visible a possible better one. To *lead* is to access and illuminate the feeling and thinking resources required to achieve the desired state. The best teachers are those who establish rapport and enter into the world of the learner to make it easier for the learner to understand the topic being taught. Joseph O'Connor and John Seymour (1990) describe this as pacing, or building a bridge between the learner's experience and yours. Having entered their world, greater permission exists for you to invite them into yours.

Effective pacing requires precision in interpreting the inner state of an audience in general-enough terms so that the speaker's statements can be regarded as accurate for most members of the group. "The people had many special skills and certain interests"; "some degree of hope existed"; "she breathed deeply as she moved into the fresh clean air" are examples of language artfully vague enough to suggest a theme but, like a radio drama, allow the listeners to make their own picture.

When should you pace? When you smell trouble—that is, audience feelings are running deep and strong enough to torpedo the objectives of the meeting. For example, a group might see a workshop as irrelevant and feel angry and frustrated at having to be there. Teachers who are assembled for a meeting might also resent being called together, and may consider the meeting a sham, their presence token, and the invitation to contribute to decision making to be a fake stone in an expensive setting. When such feelings permeate a group, the real attention in the room is subterranean; energies are below the surface, diverting power and direction from the stated purpose of the meeting.

Sometimes, as in the following situation, the pace-and-lead story can be about oneself. In this example a principal learned she was being given a new assignment—from a school on one side of town to a new, low-income, overcrowded school on the other side of town that was being formed from a school closing. It was April, and she was told she had to manage both schools until the end of the school year. People were very upset. Teachers (as well as parents and students) did not want the school closure to be happening; they were disturbed by their powerlessness and at the way the closing had occurred, and they were also apprehensive about leaving the familiar and moving to a new school.

The receiving community wasn't any happier. The following scene took place just after the decision creating the new school had been announced. About fifty unhappy people were crammed into the school library after school to meet the new principal. Some were sitting on the carpeted floor. The atmosphere was tense.

> Hello. My name is June Scofield, and I'm the principal at Pippin School across town. I've just been assigned as your new principal. I don't mind telling you that I don't want to be here. I feel dumped on. [At this point she paused and scanned the attentive faces in the room.]
>
> Let me tell you why. I'm now at a school where the staff and I have a good working relationship. We are like family, we care for one another and enjoy working hard together for the students. I know the students and parents, and we all know what to expect of each other. Things are working well, and together we're doing a good job.
>
> Now the district has told me that I need to come over here and manage this new school. Furthermore, I have to start now to begin putting it together while I am still responsible for the school I'm currently serving. I don't mind telling you, I'm upset, resentful, and I don't want to be here [pause]. I imagine many of you are feeling the same way [long pause]. I guess our job is to see what we can do to make the best transition possible.

The principal's language paced the traumatic experience of each staff member. Silence followed her opening comments, during which teachers reflected on their own experience and where the principal's comments had led them—"what we can do to make the best transition possible" (see "Signaling Your Most Important Points" in Chapter 3 for information on the potency of pausing). Griping and resistance were absent that day. Grieving was at a minimum, as the principal and teachers suspended it for this meeting in order to work productively together to identify practical next steps.

Stories to Shine Information through Defensive Structures

Adults learn by relating, comparing, and contrasting new information with previous concepts, data, and experiences. Critical to this process is receiving new information. However, information that challenges deeply held beliefs often has the effect of stacking a wall of defensive logs between the listener and the new ideas. These structures can be erected so quickly that no "sunlight," or new idea, has a chance to get through them. Sometimes a presenter's most critical job is just to get the information *heard*. In these cases, effective speakers will shine material right past the defensive logs of the listener's beliefs by aiming for the

cracks, through which the sunshine of fresh data might flow. Two approaches are used to do this. In the first, the speaker suggests a process for receiving discordant information, perhaps through anecdotes.

> How many of you saw the movie *Superman*? How about *Independence Day*? *Star Wars*? *Jurassic Park*? You may notice that when you see those kinds of films, you leave your beliefs outside the theater door. And when you come out of the theater, they are still there. You simply pick them up again, and they continue to be yours. While watching *Superman*, for example, you probably left your belief that a man can't fly outside the theater. You did that so that you could enjoy the film. If you had watched the film screening all the scenes through your belief that people don't fly, your attention would have focused on the mismatch between what you believe and what the film portrayed. All around you, people would be enjoying the movie, but you wouldn't be having any fun. I'm suggesting that today you use this same strategy of briefly suspending your beliefs, because the information I am going to present may be new, counterintuitive, or very different than what you have been taught before. You may wish to do this in order to support yourself by first taking on new information, so that you can then compare it to your existing information and experiences. I invite you to put your skepticism on hold and put your beliefs in your pocket or in a filing cabinet, knowing that you will retrieve them later to compare them with the new information you'll get here.

Another device that speakers use to get past defensive filters is to tell a story that parallels the dynamics in the problematic situation but does so at such a distance that audience members are not threatened. Helen E. Buckley's vivid poem, "The Little Boy," is one example of this (Buckley, 1961). In the poem, Buckley addresses ways of teaching children that keep them overdependent. She depicts a child's first teacher as overdirecting a class of children drawing pictures. The boy, in an initial art experience, starts to make a beautiful pink, orange, and blue flower with his crayons. The teacher corrects him, showing how to make a red flower with a green stem. While he liked his own flower much better than the teacher's, he did not say this, but just turned his paper over and made a flower like the teacher's—red with a green stem. The boy's early schooling continues like this with this teacher until he is transferred to another school. On the very first day at his new school, the teacher says, "We are going to make a picture." The poem concludes as follows:

> Good, thought the little boy,
> And he waited for the teacher
> To tell him what to do.
> But the teacher didn't say anything.
> She just walked around the room.
>
> When she came to the little boy
> She said, "Don't you want to make a picture?"
> "Yes," said the little boy. "What are we going to make?"
> "I don't know until you make it," said the teacher.
> "How shall I make it?" asked the little boy.
> "Why, any way you like," said the teacher.
> "In any color?" asked the little boy.
> "Any color," said the teacher.
> "If everyone made the same picture
> And used the same colors,
> How would I know who made what
> And which was which?"
> "I don't know," said the little boy,
> And he began to make pink and orange and blue flowers.
> He liked his new school. . . .

Stories to Alter Attitudes or Behavior

Sometimes a story allows you to say things to a group that you may not have permission to say directly. In the following situation, confidential sensing interviews had been conducted with an elementary school staff. Each person had been asked to describe the strengths and problems of the school and to make recommendations. After the interviews were completed, the group met to have the collected data presented to them. The purpose of the meeting was to identify the major problem(s) that the group wished to address and to start a problem-solving process. Just before meeting with this staff, I learned that a few teachers in the group were consistently negative, complained bitterly, blamed the principal, did not take responsibility, and usually derailed staff efforts to resolve problems. Because of this, I began the session with this story.

> Hi, I'm Bob Garmston. My job today is to give a summary report of what you said in the interviews and help you start some planning around whatever problems you'd like to solve. Before I start, though, I'm curious if any of you have read the new children's book, *How Green Is Your Garden?* [Blank faces, as the book did not, in fact, exist.] Well, let me tell you a little bit about it, because you might enjoy it. It's in a Dr. Seuss format, with wonderful pictures. It's about a gardener who lives on a very small planet, and he asks an expert from another planet to come and examine his gardening to see how well he's doing. So the expert comes in, carries a clipboard, and interviews each of the plants. As he does this, he discovers a very puzzling phenomenon: all the plants have essentially the same data, but they are reporting it in a very different way. He can't quite make out what the distinction seems to be. For example, he talks to some of the plants and they say to him [I adopted a whiny, falsetto voice], "I don't like it when the gardener waters because he floods my roots and they get all soggy and it's damp and uncomfortable, and he's a very inconsiderate gardener." The expert talks with some other plants, and they report the same data but describe it differently. [I shifted to a logical, rational tone.] "You know, I don't like it when the gardener waters, because frequently he leaves the hose unattended, water begins to flood my roots, it gets very damp and uncomfortable, and I need to let him know that. So sometimes I yell, 'Hey up there! Back off with the water, will ya?'"
>
> As the expert continues to interview the plants, he gets similar data reported in these different ways. Puzzled, he ponders on the distinctions in what he is hearing. Finally, he realizes that what is happening is that some of the plants are just complaining, while others are stating the difficulty but are taking responsibility for talking to the gardener about it in a way that makes improvement occur.

While this story was being told, the teachers' faces were like children's: open, quiet, examining, deeply attentive, knowing full well that I was talking about them; but somehow, in story format, this is permissible. The behavior in this meeting was incredibly responsive on this day. All the teachers took full responsibility for the data that was presented. They engaged productively and rationally, and in a constructive manner they identified problems to work on and suggested things that they could do.

Stories to Set and Fire Anchors

On *The Tonight Show*, Johnny Carson would wear a certain quizzical look on his face. His eyebrows furrowed, his head would tilt, and the audience would laugh. David Letterman signals to the audience that he is about to present another "Ten Best" list, and the audience laughs. On *The Carol Burnett Show*, Carol used a certain intonation to deliver a line, and we laughed.

A critical issue, whether one is teaching first graders numbers, eleventh graders botany, or school administrators shared decision-making formats, is being able to cause and maintain personal resource states. To be resourceful means to be open to learning. A *resourceful state* implies energy, attention, focus, and an "I can/I want to" learn attitude. Laughter is one of the doors to the treasure house of audience resourcefulness. In the tradition of Jack Benny (many modern comedians credit Benny as their model), Lucille Ball, Johnny Carson, Bill Cosby, and other excellent performers intuitively know that if laughter is established simultaneously with a certain look, phrase, or tonality, soon just the look or tonality will evoke the laugh. This is an example of setting and firing an anchor.

An *anchor* is a signal that evokes an internal response. For example, when you see the golden arches of the McDonald's empire, they may automatically evoke either salivation or nausea. When your loved one looks at you in a certain way or speaks to you with a certain intonation, this may generate an anchored (automatic) response. Other examples of naturally occurring anchors that evoke a pleasant response would be photographs, a favorite song, or the smell of grandmother's baking pies. The setting and firing of anchors is a common, everyday occurrence that happens without the participation of our conscious mind. Indeed, anchored responses are immediate, unconsciously learned behaviors that we reproduce whenever the original signal is presented again.

Presenters use stories to set anchors that can later be used to vividly reevoke important concepts. In the following example, a group of graduate students has been asked to design and implement a field project that breaks with the long-established tradition of setting an objective, doing linear planning, and implementing the plan in an ordered, sequential manner. Instead, they are required to lead teachers in a school improvement project where they have no predetermined solution in mind.

The problem these graduate students encounter is that after seventeen or eighteen years of formal schooling, their thinking is so locked into a linear problem-solving approach that they experience *enormous difficulty* breaking away from those mental bonds to consider this project in a fresh way. The professor tells the following story:

> Not long ago, the San Diego Zoo acquired a new bear. They were proud of this and hastened to install it in the quite delightful environment that the zoo provides for its large animals. The bears are kept in an area from which they can be seen by visitors walking along a street. There is a very low wire fence that reaches to people's waists. Beyond that is a very deep moat, and beyond that is the environment for the bears. In that setting, there is typically a large pool of water in which a bear can rest, dip, swim, and cool itself. Beyond that is a cave into which the bear can retreat for privacy and sleep, and to the left of this area, in full view of the visitors, are several trees on which the bear can sharpen its claws or scratch its back.
>
> When the persons responsible for the animals received the bear in its traveling cage, they realized, to their dismay, that this attractive environment was not yet built. They decided that the kindest thing they could do would be to put the bear, still in its traveling cage, into the center of its new home while workers completed the setting.
>
> On the first day, having been sedated for travel, the bear awoke, stretched, stood unsteadily, discovered that the movement of the cage had stopped, and began to pace slowly at first, to the right perimeter of the cage and then to the left. At each end of the cage, it rose up on its hind legs and roared. Back and forth the bear paced. The managers, seeing the apparent distress of the bear, ordered the workers to hurry so that the bear could be released as quickly as possible to its natural environment. The workers did so. And as they worked, the bear continued to pace. Two days went by, three days, four days; and the bear continued to pace in its cage. The managers, by this time becoming alarmed at the habituated behavior of the bear, ordered the workers on double time. Nearly around the clock the workers worked, until finally, on the sixth day, the environment was complete. On the next day, once again sedated so that the managers could remove the bars of the cage from around the bear, the bear awoke in its new environment. The bear stretched, stood unsteadily, and looked around. Now, with no bars between itself and its new home, the bear could see a large pool of water. Beyond that was an inviting cave, and off to the left was a pair of trees, sturdy and strong. The bear turned to its right, took three steps, and, where the edge of the cage had formerly been, rose up on its hind legs and

emitted a long and anguished roar. The bear dropped, turned, retreated to the other side where the bars had been, rose up and roared, and in this manner continued to pace back and forth in the narrow confines of its previous cage.

Later, over the course of the semester, when students are mired in old ways of thinking about their projects, the professor can refer to the "bear cage," and efforts can be marshaled to step out of their own mental restrictions.

Storytelling Style

Storytelling style is like a personal signature and, like most things about us, can be developed and learned. Speaker style can make or break a story. Patricia Fripp, the first female president of the National Speakers Association, tells us to become every character in the story we tell. By slightly changing one's voice, one's position on stage, and one's head movements, the storyteller can make each character come to life. The audience can now *see* the story as well as hear it. Fripp stresses the importance of this because "audiences don't remember what we say; they remember the pictures we created in their minds" (Fripp, 1995).

A tip on developing style is to punch up the important words in your story through inflection, gesture, and word placement. Placing the most important concept at the end of a sentence permits you to pause, then emphasize that word with the appropriate inflectional stress. For example, in the sentence, "We want to work together for student learning," if the important concept is *together,* sequence the words like this: "And so, we work for student learning—*together.*"

If, however, the most important concept is *students,* you might arrange the sentence in this sequence: "And so, we work together for the learning of—*students.*"

The "Have you ever? Well when I ..." principle is another style tip. If a presenter says, "When I was a cheerleader ..." or "When I was a football player ...", some people in the audience may listen with some resentment, contrasting their own experiences with that of the presenter. Women might think, "I was never that popular," or men might think, "I was always too small to be on the football team," and instead of developing rapport with these audience members the presenter has created some psychological distance. The same stories from personal experience can still be told, however, with a different introduction.

If the presenter says, "Have you ever had an experience so frightening that you just wanted to be anywhere else but where you were?" When participants begin nodding their heads, you know you've made a connection. "Well, let me tell you about when I was a cheerleader/quarterback/astronaut." Whatever your life is about, audience members can now connect with you across what unites us—our common human experiences—not what makes us different—our roles, body types, accomplishments.

Incongruity in speaking kills credibility and focuses audience attention on mismatches between story content and presentation. Gesture, inflection, posture, and language congruently presented with story content is very winning. Richard Nixon was a classic example of incongruity in speech. He would say, "I want to make three points about that," and then, as if responding to an echo in his own mind, a moment later he would display three fingers to the audience.

Congruity includes matching voice quality to story content. When an effective speaker talks about an exciting event, one's pitch and pace increase correspondingly. When the speaker describes certain feelings, such as sadness or pain, the voice may drop, becoming resonant and slow.

Congruity also means crediting story sources. An ounce of personal credibility is lost when speakers tell a very popular story in the first person. This causes audience attention to shift from the story to some unconscious considerations about the degree to which the speaker can be trusted.

In the final analysis, *style* means freely becoming who you are. Effective speakers may initially learn by modeling someone else, but they increasingly let go, relax, and are just themselves with an audience. They self-disclose personal mistakes. They stay light. They give primary attention to maintaining rapport with the audience. Since we each have a limited amount of memory space to bring to a presentation, our content should be so well integrated that we use none of that space for *what* we are saying but are free to concentrate all our conscious energies to monitoring and adjusting our relationship with the audience. Developing one's own presentation style is merely the process of gathering experiences and maturing in one's ability to just "be" with audiences.

As discussed in Chapter 3, style also suggests that a presenter "bring a present" to an audience. The presenter should select and wrap it with the same care that one would take in delivering a gift to a loved one. Select the gift for its value and usefulness to the audience. Keep it clothed in enough secrecy that the gift can be a surprise, and select the gift carefully to be sure that it is not something that the audience does not already have. Build anticipation and suspense, then reveal. Author Len Deighton's sentence structure ("he peeked at me over the toes of his suede shoes") is an example of allowing the meaning to become clear only at the end of the sentence (Deighton, 1962).

Storytelling is so compelling because people reason with their intuition just as much as, and perhaps more than, with their logic. Amos Tversky and Daniel Kahneman, leaders of a branch of experimental psychology called *cognitive biases*, report that in test after test with sophisticated, even scientifically trained subjects, bias for the intuitive manifests itself. "Representativeness" strongly affects our reasoning powers. That is, people are more influenced by stories (vignettes that are whole and make sense in themselves) than by data (which is, by definition, utterly abstract). (Peters and Waterman, 1982).

Anthropologist Gregory Bateson tells the following story:

> A man wanted to know about the mind—not in nature, but in his private large computer. He asked it, "Do you compute that you will ever think like a human being?" The machine then set to work to analyze its own computational habits. Finally, the machine printed its answer on a piece of paper, as such machines do. The man ran to get the answer and found, neatly typed, the words, "That reminds me of a story." Surely the computer was right; that is indeed how people think.

End Notes

Armstrong, D. (1992) *Management by Storying Around: A New Method of Leadership.* New York: Doubleday.

Peters, T. & Austin, N. (1985). *A Passion for Excellence*. New York: Random House.

Bailey, S. (1993). Stories and metaphors for change agents. Unpublished paper presented at the Association for Supervision and Curriculum Development Institute, Boston.

Buck, C. (1986). Humorless election year is nothing to laugh at. *The Sacramento Bee*, May 26.

Buckley, H. (1961). *The Little Boy*. Bradenton, FL: Helen Buckley.

Campbell, J. (1987). *Primitive Mythology: The Masks of God*. New York: Penguin.

Campbell, J. (1988). *Historical Atlas of World Mythology*. New York: Harper & Row.

Canfield, J. & Hansen, M.V. (1993). *Chicken Soup for the Soul: 101 Stories to Open the Heart and Rekindle the Spirit*. Deerfield Beach, FL: Health Communications, Inc.

Deighton, L. (1962). *The Ipcress File*. New York: Ballantine Books.

Faulkner, C. (1991). *Metaphors of Identity: Operating Metaphors and Iconic Change*. (cassette recording). Cleveland: Genesis II.

Fripp, P. (1995). *You've Got to Be Lively: Speaking Secrets of the Masters*. Harrisburg, PA: Executive Books.

Gordon, D. (1978). *Therapeutic Metaphors*. Cupertino, CA: Meta Publications.

Jones, R. (1982). *Physics As Metaphor*. New York: Meridian.

Lamb, S. (1980). Hemispheric specialization and storytelling: Implications and applications for longstanding problems. Unpublished master's thesis, University of California, Los Angeles.

Mills, J. & Crowley, R. (1986). *Therapeutic Metaphors for Children and the Child Within*. New York: Bruner/Mazel.

O'Connor, J. & Seymour, J. (1990). *Introducing Neuro-linguistic Programming: The New Psychology of Personal Excellence*. London: Mandala.

Peters, T.J. & Waterman, R.H., Jr. (1982). *In Search of Excellence: Lessons from America's Best-Run Companies*. New York: Harper & Row.

Shipley, J.T. (1959). *Dictionary of Word Origins*. Ames, IA: Littlefield, Adams & Co.

Stone, I. (1956). *Men to Match My Mountains*. New York: Doubleday.

Von Oech, R. (1983). *A Whack on the Side of the Head*. New York: Warner Books.

CHAPTER 5 The Guide's Key to Special Situations and Resources

Challenges make you discover things about yourself that you never really knew. They're what make the instrument stretch—what makes you go beyond the norm.

Cicely Tyson

Presentations offer unique challenges and frequently call for approaches that stretch us beyond the usual. The first three topics in this chapter describe some challenging circumstances and how to make them work for you and your audience. The remaining topics address some approaches to presenting that can make the difference between the ordinary and the extraordinary. In fact, they take us full circle, because they provide the final touches that support you in making presentations transformational, which was our focus in Chapter 1.

Presentation As Theater: Using Sets and Props

"Is it difficult to maintain the accent of the character you are portraying throughout the play?" someone asked. We were back stage, a small group of theater goers, interviewing an actor who had just finished a performance. "No," he said, "it's not hard, but that's not the problem with stage accents." The next thing he said startled me and caused me to wonder what similarities might exist between a stage performance and a presentation. "Audiences will develop self-actualizing hypotheses," he went on. "If the first few times you speak, they think they can't understand the character's accent, they won't be able to understand it for the rest of the play. For that reason, whenever I'm using an accent on stage, I always deliver my first lines slowly and with highly crafted enunciation. Once they believe they can understand the character, I can speak more rapidly and they still understand." How similar, I thought, to the early stages of establishing a relationship between a presenter and an audience.

I checked this perception with one of the most effective presenters I know, Michele Garside, assistant superintendent for instructional services at the Butte County Office of Education in California. Michele combines state-of-the-art knowledge about staff development, constructivist learning theory, and years on the stage in community theater. She confirms that the best presenters seem to have a flair for the theatrical. One of the manifestations of this is their careful attention to setting a stage for the presentation or workshop and in their creative use of audiovisual aids. These aides can quite properly be considered stage "props" and can add luster, interest, and focus to a well-crafted speech or workshop. They can also enhance retention. This section explores the use of some common and not-so-common tools that presenters use for these purposes.

Take Time to Set the Stage

Michele reminded me that the presentation always starts before you do. When your audience enters the presentation room, what they initially see and hear begins their learning experience. The set, the accumulation of onstage accouterments within which the performance will be played, typically includes a screen (depicted as A in Figure 5.1) and two flip charts (B). The screen serves as the central focusing point in the presentation and the flip charts mark the edge of the stage. The central performances will occur within that space. If flip charts cannot be found, portable display walls, chalkboards, or tall potted plants can mark the left and right boundaries of the stage. The table in the center (C) becomes a location for the overhead projector and a prop table for those overheads, markers, script prompts, and other items the presenter wants close at hand. Overhead projector carts should be used *only* for transport. They provide an inadequate working space for the speaker. The table behind the screen (D) is a place to spread out and organize those props that will be used less frequently and those that may be optionally used. Two high presentation stools (E) serve as alternative locations in which the presenter may be seated and still give the audience full visual access to him or her. For audiences larger than 150 or so, a set of risers on which the above items can be placed helps the audience to see.

Figure 5.1: Setting the Stage

After arranging the set, skillful presenters check the sight lines, moving to various parts of the room, sitting in audience seats, and making adjustments to ensure that each participant can easily see (and hear) the performer. Depending on the purposes and instructional design of the "performance," presenters will sometimes arrange the furniture so that audience members can also easily see and interact with each other. A final check ensures that the presenter has clear walk lines, providing ease of movement within the audience.

What the audience hears as they enter the room is also an important part of the set. Just as lighting and music on a stage develop mood before the play begins, before-the-opening music can set a welcoming tone and invite relaxation. Music affects the emotions, respiratory system, heart rate, brain waves, and overall learning capacity of your audience. Baroque music at sixty beats per minute is often associated with programs of accelerated learning. For imagery and relaxation, consider New Age artists such as Steven Halpern, Georgia Kelly, George Winston, and the classic *Canon in D* by Johann Pachebal. For a mellow energizer, try a Mozart concerto. For light jazz, try Joe Sample, Dave Gruisan, Bob James, or Earl Klugh.

Using the Set

In the theater, actors occupy various stage locations for specific purposes. They sit or stand to add visual interest for the audience, and they may reserve a specific location on the set for certain types of communications, like delivering soliloquies. When doing *Hamlet*, for example, notice that the director will usually have the actor move to the same place on the stage to represent reflection and inner dialogue. In a similar manner, presenters will sometime reserve a portion of the set as a place from which to tell stories, another location from which they can change character and deliver data, and perhaps a third from which they become a colleague and engage in informal conversations with the audience. This presentation stance is often played from one of the presentation stools or by sitting, legs dangling, on top of the center prop table (C). Many presenters will move to a designated spot on the set to make comments to the audience about processes that they are using.

Having set the stage, the presenter also has the option of working off the set to give special emphasis to certain ideas. In Chapter 3, we discussed "out-there" pointing: moving to a wall and pointing beyond it to talk about some negative ideas that other people "out there" might have. This eloquent stage move ensures that audience members do not think you are talking about them when you are discussing counterproductive attitudes or behavior. I use this principle when I move "off stage" to give a counterexample about the directions for an activity.

Select and Place Props with Care

Michele tells me that when a director works with props, great care is taken in the selection and placement of the prop on the stage or in a waiting area. Each prop must enhance the production. Nothing should be onstage or on a prop table that does not have a purpose in being there. In presentations, good presenters intuitively follow this principle by initially removing clutter from the presentation space. Between "scenes" they act as crew, cleaning up, rearranging how charts are hung, and straightening furniture.

A set is sedentary, whereas a prop is movable. Sometimes the same item can serve as both. For example, a chair that is part of the set onstage can be shifted to center stage, turned around, and straddled sideways to illustrate an informal posture in a conversation. It thus becomes a prop. Or, the two presentation stools (E) that are part of the set in Figure 5.1 can be placed facing each other to illustrate two persons talking to one another.

Overheads, of course, are props, and much has been written about their effective use (Smith, 1984). A recent discovery of mine is that slides or color photos can be transferred to an overhead transparency format, bringing color, and therefore interest, to a presentation without the fuss and inflexibility of working with slides. Fewer images of this type are more effective than many images. Too many can become a visual handicap, making the presentation disjointed and making people forget the structure of the speech while looking at the pictures. Some presenters recommend no more than seven overheads for a fifty-minute talk. Each transparency, even if it contains no more than one picture or half a dozen key words, is usually enough for five to ten minutes of speaking.

Little has been written about flip-chart markers. Here are a few tips. When working with audiences of 150 persons or more, a large, broad-tipped pen is useful in charting key words as visual organizers for a portion of your talk. For example, in introducing an unfamiliar term, you might print (avoid cursive—it's harder to read) three words—what, why, and how—as an advance organizer for your comments. Two brands of pens give fairly good service. Sanford's Magnum 44 Marker is good but has the disadvantage of being permanent ink. Sakura's water-based SG7 Extra Broad Marker is also good but is limited in color choices. For normally sized chart pens, Paper Mate's Marker, in ten brilliant water-based colors, cannot be beat. To the best of my knowledge, these are only sold through Interaction Associates Inc., 600 Townsend Street, #550, San Francisco, CA 94103, (415) 241–8010. Sanford's Mr. Sketch pens are okay and are the best substitute for Paper Mate, but suffer from limited color choice and brilliance, and the tips wear out more quickly. Incidentally, a yard-stick, correction tape and Pentel's correction pen (a liquid white-out) are handy tools to carry in your prop bag for your before-the-session chart making.

A brief word on flip charts. There are some absolutely terrible ones on the market. What you want are firm, sturdy charts that hold a paper size of 27 x 34 inches. Two good makes are Chartpak Easel Model No. E60 and Oravisual Model A502, which add the attribute of easy portability.

To focus visual attention on overheads, the Learning Resource's Transparent Counters are excellent (Lincolnshire, IL: LER 131, 250 Counters). Three-quarter inch circles come in six colors. They also make a collection of transparent geometric shapes that can be used for this purpose.

Signal systems represent another form of presentation prop. I'm partial to a set of chimes made of three metal bars of graduated length mounted on a block of wood. The only place I know of today to get these chimes is at J. W. Stannard Company in Largo, Florida (800–822–4964). They cost about $29. Other auditory signaling devices include train whistles and bicycle bells. Of course, as the presenter, you are also a prop, and hand claps, your raised hand, and other devices in which you use your own body in a patterned way can also become a "signature" signal for an event.

Hardly any conversation I have about expert presenters is complete without Suzanne Bailey's name coming up. Michele told me how Suzanne will use people cutouts as props. Three-foot-high butcher-paper human figures are distributed. Participants are asked, "Who else needs to be in the room to do this work?" Children, board members, or parents are examples of groups that participants might name. On the cutouts they draw faces, write attributes, and perhaps list the questions that these person would pose if they were present. This activity brings the presence of these persons into the room and broadens the perspective through which audience members construct their learning.

The Ultimate Prop

You, of course, are always your most important audiovisual aid. Your clothes and grooming make a statement to the audience, and within the first few minutes, that statement speaks. Michele advises that if you are given a choice between dressing up or down, dress up. Whatever teachers wear in the classroom to teach is appropriate there, but in front of a group of adults it may often appear inappropriate. Remember, from the perspective of presentation as theater, you're wearing a costume when you enter the presentation room.

Making Nervousness Work for You

Notes from a Safari Journal

Several times now we've seen it—perhaps the most nervous creature out here. Juma says it's called a bat-eared fox. Its ears are enormous; they are black-edged and oval, and Juma says the fox uses them to *Hear* insects, for goodness' sake, which it eats. Very skittish, its head pops up over the tall grass, it looks intently at us, and then whoosh—it's gone. It keeps the fox safe, I guess. Also, Juma says, the fox has to keep moving to get enough food because the insects are not territorial.

Part of my mind says that the title of this section is as unlikely a one as I've ever written. My first reaction to nervousness is frequently to wish it away, hide it, or overcome it. Another part of my being knows that when I dance with my own nervousness, I can use its energy to fuel my planning and performance, and I can ultimately transcend its debilitating effects.

The experience of nervousness is universal. Figure 5.2 shows some of the manifestations of nervousness. Often, being observed by others, or just the prospect of being observed, creates a keyed-up state in which adrenalin increases, the heart beats faster, breathing rates increase, pupils dilate, and response time quickens. Both novices and professional performers experience it, even some of the world's most famous presenters. All this can be a plus when properly utilized. It helps the speaker to meet the demands of speaking, and it has an energizing effect that can improve performance.

Sources of Nervousness

According to C. Turk (1985), there are six major sources of presentation nervousness: (1) audience size, (2) audience importance, (3) speaker familiarity with the audience, (4) difficulty of the subject, (5) vulnerability of the presenter's public persona, and (6) experience of the speaker.

Large audiences often seem more intimidating than small ones. Also, the degree of importance that the speaker assigns to the audience affects nervousness. I worked once with a military man who gave regular briefings to Ronald Reagan when he was president of the United States. The man's rehearsals were lengthy and intense, and his nervousness quotient was understandably

sweating
dry mouth
rapid heartbeat
yawning repeatedly
short breath
inability to speak loudly
tense, tight throat
tense face
tense body
butterflies in stomach
nauseous feeling
weak knees
coldness
itchy or twitchy feeling
high-pitched voice
rapid speech

Figure 5.2: Signs of Nervousness and Physical Distress

very high. The better known the group is to the speaker, the more predictable they are, and the less presenter apprehension there is likely to be. If the topic is difficult for the audience to comprehend or difficult for the speaker to talk about (e.g., if it is the first time the speaker is presenting this material), the speaker will experience more nervousness.

Being overly concerned with how you will look to others guarantees anxious feelings and reduction of resourcefulness. Whenever one becomes concerned about looking good, smart, well-informed, or not looking clumsy or irrelevant, the butterflies mass, take off, and vengefully fly out of control. Whenever we try, in other words, to be something we are not, the risk factor goes up and pulls anxiety with it. Finally, the most anxiety-producing source of all is lack of experience. Fortunately, it is also the factor we can do the most to correct.

What causes these sensations of distress? The hormone adrenalin is the major player in creating these symptoms. As you know, the purpose of adrenalin is to help us survive attack.

When the hippopotamus went after me in the Ngorongoro Crater, you can bet I had plenty of adrenalin pumping through my system. In that setting, the adrenalin surge was totally functional. Chemically, it alerts my brain and my body to be prepared for fight or flight. My heart beats faster; muscles tense, preparing me for physical exertion; blood leaves my extremities; a coagulating process occurs in my blood for protection against injury; and, in extreme cases, I can get nauseous or even vomit. Even throwing up has a purpose. In prehistoric days, when humans were still largely hunters and gathers, food supplies were not always dependable. So when food was available, they gorged. Since outrunning a saber-tooth tiger is incompatible with the process of digesting food, the food on those occasions was disgorged. That biological and historical information doesn't help us deal with the jitters in today's speech—or does it? Actually, the realization that the adrenalin puts our mind and body in sync for perceived danger can be useful.

Seven Tips

You can make the state of nervousness your ally by imagining that, like the bat-eared fox, the purpose of its presence is to protect you and support you in doing a job of which you'll feel proud. This is an extension of a principle from the Japanese martial art of *aikido*. *Aikido*, literally translated, means "the way of blending energy" (Crum, 1987). From this perspective, all of life, including presentation anxiety, is simply energy with which to dance. Since nervous energy is a mental phenomenon with physiological results, presenters can achieve desired states of calm by employing techniques of mental and/or physical preparation.

Because body and mind are connected, treatment of one addresses the other. What follows are seven tested techniques for converting nervousness; four of them are physical, three of them are mental. I invite you to explore these, and develop the personal patterns that are best suited to you.

1. **Breathe** This is the simplest and possibly most effective relaxation technique. Just before you present take three deep breaths. They should be full and slow, all the way down, filling the lungs. Concentrate on your breathing. Think of nothing else. Just three good deep breaths are enough. They add oxygen to the system, distract your attention from fear, and help clear the mind.
2. **Do progressive relaxation** Tense and relax your body, part by part. For example, first tense the toes and then

relax them. Then tense your feet and relax them; then do the ankles, and so on.

3. **Walk** Notice that athletes walk and stretch prior to performances. This warms up not only the muscles but also the psyche. Walking vigorously just prior to your presentation uses adrenalin, gets oxygen into the body, and relaxes the large muscles.

4. **Center yourself physically** When you are centered, you become more in touch with who you are and less dependent on outside approval. The centered state is simple, natural, and powerful. Following is one way of centering yourself (for others see Crum, 1987). Stand. Allow both arms to drop naturally to your sides. Have your feet spread so that they are appropriately balanced beneath you. Take some long, deep breaths. With each slow exhalation, imagine that you see the tension flowing out of your body from head to toe. Allow your spine to lengthen; mentally reach toward your hair and pull a strand of it up so that your neck is elongated and your spine is comfortably stretched. Now, from this position, sway slightly back and forth for ten to fifteen seconds, gradually decreasing the size of the sway till you reach center. Now imagine that you are pushing both feet into the floor, then release. Your body will let you know when you have that centered feeling from which your presentation can take place.

Experienced presenters use presession nervousness as a signal to take special care in planning. As suggested earlier, the greatest stress producer is lack of experience. The next three strategies help overcome this.

5. **Overprepare** All "butterfly redirection" starts with planning. Be very clear and particular about your opening. If this is a special occasion and you are feeling some extra nervousness, memorize the first seven minutes so that you can deliver these lines even if your mental space closes down. Plan to stand still during the opening so people can "measure" you.

6. **Write notes** Write down what you plan to say. Rewrite it and simplify it. Some may want to mind-map it. Rewrite it again. Continue to rewrite it, organize it, and list it until it is finally in very succinct form, with each idea that is written on the paper automatically triggering in your mind the related ideas that you wish to present on that section.

7. **Mentally rehearse** Bruce Wellman and I believe (Garmston and Wellman, 1992) that rich mental rehearsal, along with the first two mental techniques, will redirect 80 percent of most people's nervousness. Much has been written on the topic of mental rehearsal. We are learning from the athletic community how rich envisioning creates what is known as the Carpenter effect: this causes nerves, muscles, and the entire body to behave as if they have experienced an actual practice. This technique has been successfully employed with athletes in team and individual sports and with peak performers in leadership roles. Fortunately, the technique also works in the complex and interactive areas such as teaching, facilitating, and presenting. There are three keys to good mental imagery: (1) create rich (visual, auditory, kinesthetic) internal representations, (2) make adjustments until they feel right, and (3) make the representations from your perspective as well as the audience's perspective.

   For example, imagine yourself preparing to present a topic to a group in the near future. Close your eyes. Take three deep breaths. See yourself in the room. Notice the way your body is organized in space. If you are standing, notice your posture. Notice where your feet are on the floor in relationship to your shoulders above them. Notice the placement of your hands and the expression on your face. From an audience's perspective, what would they see on your face? Where would your eyebrows be–raised or lowered? What degree of animation do you have? What would they hear? Notice the pitch and the rhythm of your voice. Listen to the patterns of your speech. Hear what you say. Be aware of the amount of floor space that you are using, your gestures, your walk, how you handle the overheads. Now step into your own body in that picture and sense what it feels like. Make any adjustments that you might need in order to have the feeling

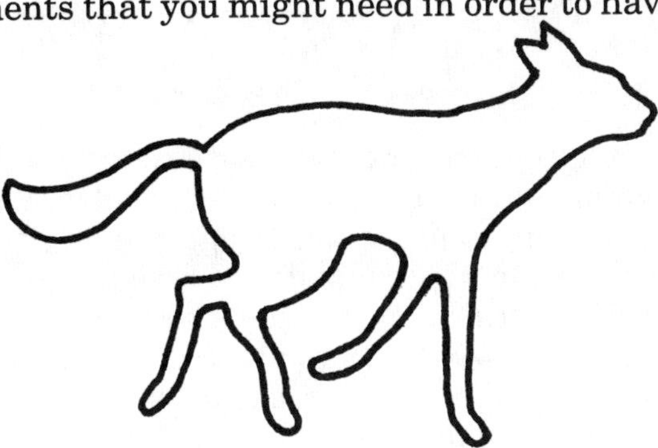

be correct. Keep watching the audience and your own performance and continue making the adjustments until they are exactly the way you want them.

Mental rehearsal does not take long. It's possible to rerun a rehearsal film, making adjustments several times. Each time you run the film, your body responds as if you had actually been there. What was unfamiliar becomes familiar. What is familiar becomes predictable. What is predictable lacks anxiety-producing elements.

Celebrating Resistance

Mutiny! Yellow post-its were everywhere: on the backs of chairs, on the door to the men's room. "Remember!" "Let's do it."

These were secretive reminders to be disruptive in the morning session, to whisper, and to be otherwise inattentive when my copresenter (Suzanne Bailey) and I began to present. For many participants, their planned behavior of resistance went uninitiated, and for others the behavior they executed went unnoticed.

What happened? We didn't resist. Since resistance persists only within systems of resistance, the intentions of these adults to test their disruptive powers and study our reactions failed to even get off the ground. Incidentally, we were honored by their trust and their gumption to work on such a bold experiment during our three-day workshop on Becoming a State-of-the-Art Presenter.

Resistance to change and learning is common. Following are some concepts and strategies drawn from the literature on psychology, hypnosis, group dynamics, and personal experience.

First, let's consider the type of system that resistance needs in order to live. Run water through the hose. Knot the hose: instant resistance. Untie the knot, and the water once again flows through its natural course.

A participant voices a complaint. We counter with logic. We knot the hose; or we paraphrase, openly listening without defensiveness, without explaining our behavior, and the water flows freely. Resistance can only exist when we resist the resistance. To bypass the resistance, break the system.

Lipshitz, Friedman, and Omer (1989) believe that resistance is a "positive, healthy reaction that enables people to maintain stability under extremely turbulent conditions." They offer several strategies that are designed to infiltrate behind the lines, interject new ideas, and facilitate change. The following are two of my favorites.

Assuming a One-Down Position

> I don't pretend to be a better mathematics teacher than you. While my work has led to an understanding of which cognitive processes separate the high-achieving from the low-achieving student, and while I know a lot of specific ways to teach the low-achieving student some strategies that will increase his or her performance, I cannot begin to know the particular circumstances and students with whom you work. Please bear with me if I offer some things that are inappropriate; adopt those that will work for you and advise me of where I might strengthen my knowledge base.

The intent of this type of statement is to shift the focus from the presenter's expertise to the participant's expertise and to eliminate possible power struggles.

Preempting

Another prevention strategy that Lipshitz, Friedman, and Omer (1989) offer involves anticipating a difficulty or an emotional block that participants may have in completing an assignment. The presenter foreshadows this and gives the impression that it is a normal expectation of learning and that it will serve as only a temporary and not a serious barrier. The presenter then offers tips about how to overcome it.

> Some of you may notice that as you begin to incorporate these skills in your teaching, you may actually get worse before you get better. Your mind may offer compelling arguments to stop the innovation because it's interfering with your effectiveness. This is a very natural part of the process of growth—even your own admonition to quit—and will not last very long.
>
> There are at least two things you can do to prepare for this: (1) be willing to live through a brief period of discomfort, and (2) select just a part of this new teaching technique to practice each day. Over-rehearse it until it becomes second nature.

Both strategies include principles of hypnotic suggestion pioneered by Milton Erickson. In each, the presenter has anticipated and incorporated potential resistance into the instruction. Should resistance emerge, it will feel to the participant like part of the instructions. It seems, therefore, not to be resistance at all but a form of cooperation with the presenter. To do this effectively, the presenter's language must be artfully vague, letting each participant tailor his or her own suit of understandings from the fabric of language given to all.

But even with all your skills, in some audiences there may be 1 or 2 percent of the people whose major pleasure is to see you fail. Whatever you do, they will be able to find fault. Perhaps you speak too quickly or too slowly. Perhaps your clothes clash with the color scheme of the setting. It's somewhat reassuring to know that whatever you do, you will help these people reach their goal.

The Language of Offense

I talk to teach, yet when I carelessly offend, I teach what I do not intend.

I am white, American-born and male. I am, or have been, a teacher, administrator, and professor. These accidents of birth and role both open and close me to experiences, viewpoints, and frames of mind. I am usually careful when I make presentations to avoid unintentionally offending others through carelessness in my language or insensitivity to their perspectives.

However, during a painfully memorable presentation in a midsize school district, I learned more about how little I know about my own language of offense. My teachers were four persons of another race, and one of my own. In gentle and skillful ways, these people courageously caused me to become aware of how some clever and "innocent" lines were, for most of the audience, furthering unconscious acceptance of stereotypes and, for some of the audience, wounding and breaking the learning momentum as they went inside themselves to engage in internal dialogue and feelings. I had lost the attention of these persons to the topic on which I was presenting.

"No more Indian jokes, huh?!" the man smiled, as he gave me a bear hug at the morning break. I had used a line I learned long ago, and with a delivery polished through testing with many audiences: "You know how generalizations are formed? All Indians walk single file ... [pause] ... at least the only one I ever saw did." Nothing in the surface structure of this sentence is derogatory, yet to a member of any ethnic minority group, a rightful sensitivity exists to the use of minority characters in puns, jokes, or anecdotes.

"You know, we're not objects to be beaten!" confided a woman after I had given another of my favorite lines illustrating the use of presupposition, or hidden meanings, in language. "An early example of presupposition comes from the old vaudeville line, 'when did you stop beating your wife?'; now, what is presupposed there?" Surprised, at first, at this woman's reaction to this "innocent" line, I began to realize the deepest presuppositions in that vaudeville story (endured by appalling numbers of women who are trapped in relationships of brutality)—women are to be beaten. The line "innocently," and out of conscious awareness, supports that point of view. The fact that the presenter's communication slips beyond conscious awareness is very important, for that is the channel of deepest and uncontested learning (O'Hanlon, 1987).

Nor are occupation or role groups immune to our unintentional verbal battering. Disrespectful asides about salespersons and lawyers are often heard by presenters. What happens to the teacher in the audience who is married to an attorney? How do you think he or she feels when the lawyer joke is told?

So what? Isn't a joke just a joke? At least three implications of the unintentionally abusive comment come to mind.

First, a slight on any subgroup diminishes us all. If I can laugh at them, by inference I can, and may, laugh at you. Each group—liberal, fundamentalist, gay, board member, teacher-union officer, Hispanic, Asian, black, white (and *which* Hispanic, Asian, black, or white culture, specifically?) has a group history and a language, and each member of each group has a personal history that compellingly contribute to certain well-formed and well-intentioned points of view, values, and perceptions. To be disrespectful of the experience from which other people have derived meaning and behavior is to be egocentrically nearsighted and to devalue who we are and how we learn.

A second implication of such comments is that stereotyping groups—any group—contributes to less understanding, deepens our human and cultural isolation, and inhibits our ability to resolve complex problems in a multifaceted world.

A third implication is of immediate concern to the presenter. Just as four-letter words are guaranteed to offend some audience members, comments that put down one sex, race, or group are guaranteed to break the momentum of attention and learning for those audience members who identify directly or indirectly with the subgroup mentioned.

So what can we say to make our points? I've been thinking about how to revise some of my old presentation lines. How about "All muskrats walk in single file ... [pause] ... at least the only one I ever saw did," or "When did you stop feeding the unicorn?" What are the presuppositions there?

I used to have a habit of saying "guys" in a generic way, encompassing everyone in the audience. Recently, a principal brought me a note at break time asking me to monitor that language, since two of his teachers were disturbed by it and their being upset was diverting him from the topic. Although I had been aware for several years of this gender-biased language pattern of mine, I could come up with no language alternative that was acceptable to my ears. Well, getting that note was embarrassing enough that I started to pay attention. I'm saying "folks" now, though it seems appropriate in only some regions of the country, and if I catch myself saying "guys," I will add, "and gals." A little pain sometimes helps. Maybe we can all help each other by offering data like this.

The Listening Presenter

Notes from a Safari Journal

We are rolling along at a steady clip. The viewing roof of the Land Rover is raised. It's hot, all windows are open, and we are catching as much wind as we can. Standing, I lower my voice to say something confidential to Sue. Juma, up in the driver's seat, eyes on the road and hands on the wheel, responds. Repeatedly, I can't believe how sensitive he is to every sound and how he listens intently to our experiences. Both Sue and I are impressed with how much he is there for us.

I was surprised recently when a participant in a seminar told me that my listening was the most important part of the presentation to her. After all, my job *is* to present, to deliver communications, isn't it? In fact, I sometimes tease audiences with an old line taught to me by Dick Suchman, the originator of Inquiry Training. "My job *is* to present, yours is to listen. If you get through before I do, please let me know."

As I reflected on her comment, however, I realized that listening is an important part of what we do when we present. In what follows, I explore why listening is important and how to monitor and improve your presentation listening.

The Benefits of Listening

An optimum learning environment is one in which individuals participate fully in the presentation experience without pretense or artifice. They feel free to be themselves; to know or not know; to have opinions; to admit fatigue, boredom, or lack of understanding; or to say that they are thirsty or have to go to the bathroom. An optimum learning environment is one in which participants feel safe: safe enough to form bonds with others, to develop community, to take charge of their learning, to question, to challenge, and to risk the discomfort that sometimes accompanies rich learning by publicly living at the edge of their own competence and knowledge. An ideal learning environment is one in which participants feel recognized and valued (because they are) for their resources, noble intentions, and individuality.

When you present, you do many things to develop such an environment. Of all that you do, however, perhaps the most unexamined is listening.

Honest listening conveys that you are attempting to understand. This is a more potent message than "I understand," because to *attempt* to understand communicates that you value the participant. Listening shifts the audience's attention from the presenter to the audience member, who is another expert or inquirer in the room, or, better yet, draws attention to the relationship between the two of you. Listening invites the audience to witness a dialogue, an unscripted and unpredictable event, and, therefore, one that is very energizing because no one knows how it will end. Finally, listening reveals the presenter; it illuminates the person behind the role and the practiced show.

How to Listen to an Audience Member

Here are five principles of presenter listening that are used by premier speakers and presenters. You might use this list as a self-check or ask a friend to watch for these patterns the next time you are presenting.

- **Stop and Look**

  Stop whatever you are doing. Stand still. Look fully and attentively at the speaker. Make eye contact. These attending behaviors signal your willingness and desire to hear and understand what the speaker has to say. Empty your mind of the desire to develop responses. Prepare to listen.

- **Listen Verbally and Nonverbally**

  All behavior in an interactional situation has message value, so give your fullest attention to the speaker as he or she proceeds. Allow your body to reflect your understanding—nodding, smiling, or grimacing, as appropriate. Listeners unconsciously construct enormous meaning from a speaker's nonverbal behaviors. In fact, one theory about nonverbal signals is that "language evolved and is normally used for communicating information about events external to the speakers, while the nonverbal code is used, by humans and by nonhuman primates, to establish and maintain personal relationships" (Turk, 1985).

  Also use the verbal skills of reflective listening, providing wait time and paraphrasing. Nonjudgmentally ask the speaker to clarify terms, phrases, or concepts that are unfamiliar to you. A caution here is that when listening, your responses to the speaker should constitute about 10 percent or less of the verbal interaction between you.

- **Punctuate Responses**

  Presenters punctuate to add meaning and clarity to speech. They punctuate when they use unfilled pauses (silence) and filled pauses (ahs and ums). They punctuate by using nonverbal marks, such as moving to new floor space or using hand signals to separate purposes (now I'm listening, now I'm answering a question), thoughts (some authors take this position, others take that position), relationships (now I'm facilitating your thinking and am expressing no opinion, now I'm offering an opinion), and ideas (here are three ideas, first, second, and third).

  Three punctuations are universally useful in listening to audience members: the pause before responding, which gives you time to reflect and simultaneously models thinking behaviors; the movement to a new place in the room to begin your response to the speaker; and the use of the speaker's name. Above all else, I have learned that speaking to people by name generates mutual respect and makes the presentation room a more friendly climate. If I don't know a name, I ask. If I can't pronounce it on the first try, I keep trying, requesting corrections. Everyone's name is difficult for someone to pronounce. I'm most frequently called *Bob.* Recently, in the South Pacific, the closest most people could come to that was *Bobpt.* It still made me feel good to be "recognized."

- **Acknowledge**

  Because I conduct seminars on presenting, I often get rich feedback from audiences on my own behavior. It never ceases to amaze me how important it is for audience members to get a simple *thank you, yes,* or a respectful *uh huh* from the presenter after offering a comment.

- **Decide What to Do Next**

  At this point there are several options. You might exit the dialogue, entertaining conversation from someone else or returning to your presentation stance. Your use of the previous principle, a simple acknowledgment, is a way to do this. You may utilize the speaker's comment to underscore and return to your theme. You may choose to seize this as a teaching opportunity and conduct a minilecture. You may choose to answer a question inferred from the speaker's comment. To explore other ideas on answering questions, see "Responding to Questions" in Chapter Three.

How Not to Listen

As obvious as it may seem, most of the tips on how not to listen are the opposites of the preceding list. I've watched some knowledgeable and well-intentioned presenters, however, quickly lose audience rapport through their listening behaviors. Here are some of the more damaging patterns.

I stress the word *patterns,* because these behaviors in isolation are not counterproductive. In fact, at times they may be called for and useful. As patterns of listening, however, they seem to communicate that this is not a dialogue, it is a show, or worse yet, it is an "I get you to talk so I can say what I want to say" ploy.

- **Always Adding**

  Whatever is said, the presenter usually has something to add. Frequently this begins to appear as if the presenter is attempting to demonstrate his or her own knowledge.

- **Interrupting**

  Beyond bad manners, this is perceived as impatience, and most of the time it reveals your incomplete understanding of the person's points. Interrupting is appropriate, however, when you need to check your hearing or understanding, or if you've diagnosed a pattern of verbal diarrhea.
- **Checking Your Notes, Overhead, Shoelaces, Etc.**

  Anything that takes your full, undivided attention away from the speaker communicates a devaluation of what is being said. This includes pointless movements, repetitively shifting your weight from one foot to the other, behaving like a pacing tiger, or unconscious patterns such as pencil twirling. In fact, any movement that is not related to your listening is distracting to an audience. The same is true, of course, when you are speaking.
- **Debating**

  Repetitive debate suggests several possibilities. One, you may not be listening, and this is what is being communicated to your audience. Two, you do not have regard for the views of others. Three, you are trying too hard to "sell" your position or program. I've learned that whenever I get so impassioned in what I'm presenting that I began to "sell," I've lost my effectiveness. The presenter's job is to invite exploration and expand choices. The "salesperson" in me often awakes "sales resistance" in you. Then we've both stopped listening.

  In a sense, one could describe listening by borrowing a metaphor of Henry Ford's about money. He said that money is extremely simple; it is part of our transportation system. It is a simple and direct method of conveying goods from one person to another.

  So, too, is listening.

Paddling Together: A Copresenting Primer[4]

Copresenters resemble two paddlers piloting a canoe downstream. Both need to agree on a destination and continually monitor the direction to make sure that they're still going where they want to go. Deftly, they correct, correct, correct—paddling

[4]The original form of this section appeared as an article in *Training and Development* with coauthor Suzanne Bailey (Garmston and Bailey, 1988). It has been reprinted with permission. All rights are reserved.

on this side, then on that. At times, paddles at rest, they may recalculate the goal itself. Is the destination that was agreed to ten minutes ago still appropriate?

It's an intricate process and, done well, it's extremely rewarding. Done poorly, it produces calluses and a colossal pain right where the canoeist meets the bottom of the boat. Since so many people experience more pain than pleasure in copresenting, why try it at all?

After two years of copresenting, Suzanne and I had begun to understand how to maximize the pleasures and minimize the pains that are inherent in this valuable presentation method. We found that the pleasures can be bountiful for both trainees and copresenters. My experiences since that time with a host of talented copresenters have deepened my appreciation of this form of teaching.

Accentuating the Positive

Copresenting improves almost any training effort in several ways. It adds to the energy that trainers bring to their presentations. It lets each presenter come to the other's rescue when necessary. Payoffs for session participants include better training designs, increased diversity, and the benefits that come from the behavior that copresenters model while they train.

Presenting is hard work, so the energy factor is an important one. Presenters who work by themselves manage many cognitive tasks at the same time—monitoring audience reaction, keeping track of content, managing time. Copresenters benefit by conserving personal energy. In copresenting, neither person is "on" all the time. While one speaks, the other can perform important presentation functions, such as assessing the audience or planning modifications in the lesson. Copresenters also benefit by drawing energy from one another. Watch any TV news show and notice how the banter between the anchorpersons contributes to their liveliness and energy.

Copresenters can also come to each other's rescue. Presenters tell us that one of their biggest fears is going blank in the middle of a presentation. When one copresenter goes blank or gets off track, the partner can come in with needed corrections.

Increased energy levels and the come-to-the-rescue factor both help presenters. But if copresenting benefited only the presenters, it would be hard to justify the costs. Copresenting also considerably benefits trainees.

Participants benefit because they usually get a much better training design. Copresenters can test ideas with one another and reassess direction and strategy during initial planning and during the presentation. I recall a session in which Suzanne and I had planned a ninety-minute presentation on copresenting for consultants. We thought we had developed a reasonable design for teaching this topic, but one of us felt uncomfortable with the plan. After we discussed it, we realized we had based our entire design on some faulty assumptions about what information the consultants needed to know. We identified more appropriate assumptions and reworked the design. The resulting product was much more useful.

Participants also benefit from the diversity, variety, and richness that two presenters bring to a session. They get variety in personality, approach to the topic, and presentation style. They also get audio relief. When we copresent, trainees get the benefit of more than eighty years of experience. We bring the sum of our total lives to the training room, and who we are, our values, and our ways of being are more persuasive than anything we say.

In addition, participants get closer monitoring, and from this they get more advocacy for their needs and interests. Two people are available for break-time chats with participants, and both can follow up on individual concerns. Two sets of antennae are alert for participant needs.

Copresenting rivets group-member attention. Participants focus on both presenters individually, the interaction between them, and the session visuals. In a positive sense, a two-person presentation resembles a circus—so much goes on at any one time that the conscious mind can't take it all in. Copresenters who are skilled in metaphor, suggestion, and other forms of accelerated learning can use this perceptual overload to accelerate trainee acquisition of skills and knowledge.

Modeling between copresenters also reinforces the presentation message. Here the canoe metaphor is particularly apt: it communicates a real relationship. The play—the collegial relationship—between copresenters reveals itself to participants on conscious and subconscious levels. The statement that this relationship makes—dramatized in front of participants for their right brains to see, feel, and communicate to their analytical left brains—may be the most eloquent and persuasive statement made in the training room. The more copresenters operate synchronistically, as in a dance, the more powerful this subliminal message, and the more enjoyable and productive the learning experience.

Forms of Copresenting

Copresenting can take five main forms: tag-team, speak-and-comment, speak-and-chart, perform-and-comment, and duet.

- **Tag-Team**

  In this style of copresenting, presenters take turns: one is on while the other is off. Many find this method the best for beginning a copresenting relationship. It also works well for delivering new material that one or both presenters have not yet internalized.

Working at this level, one copresenter monitors the audience as an extra set of eyes and ears while the other delivers the material. Those new to training will find that tag-team presentations allow them to train at higher levels than they could before. Teams get richer data about audience responses for use in their post-training debriefing.

- **Speak-and-Comment**

  This form of copresenting puts both presenters on stage at the same time. One makes a statement and the other adds to it. One leads; the other supports.

  The leader is in charge of the content and makes process decisions—when to move on, end discussions, or proceed to the next content area. The supporter does whatever is necessary to achieve the goals of the particular session segment. He or she may add humor if the leader gets too dry, rub the shoulders of sleepy participants, or move props. This is the beginning, and the easiest, level of spontaneous broadcasting. Speak-and-comment lets copresenters capitalize on their different perspectives and experiences.

- **Speak-and-Chart**

  This method extends speak-and-comment. Using speak-and-chart, the leader presents content and elicits participant comments, while the supporter records participant or copresenter ideas on a flip chart or overhead transparency. The supporter acts as the session's neutral and invisible documenter. Successful speak-and-chart presentations demand the following critical attributes:

1. Both presenters must clearly understand who plays which role.
2. The leader must monitor the accuracy and speed with which the supporter records.
3. The recorder must summarize spoken ideas quickly without distorting concepts or vocabulary.
4. The recorder must remain silent and neutral.

The speak-and-chart method works powerfully because 40 percent of people report that they best absorb information visually. In contrast, only 20 percent report auditory processing as their preferred method of learning—and audiences can reach auditory overload very quickly. Thus, visual aids improve participant learning. They also help participants develop a group memory, to which they and the copresenters can return as needed.

- **Perform-and-Comment**

  Art Costa and I discovered that audiences will sometimes observe what is irrelevant in skills demonstrations unless we help them focus their efforts at data collection. By assigning observation roles to pairs or trios, we can assist participants to not only see and hear greater details, but also to examine interactions and relationships.

  For example, to learn more about the potency of questioning in a Cognitive Coaching[sm] seminar, the performing partner might demonstrate an unrehearsed conference with an audience member. The second partner has instructed members of trios to record their observations on either (1) the questions asked by the coach, (2) evidence of teacher thinking as manifested by verbal or nonverbal responses, or (3) the essence of the relationship between coach and coachee.

  The second partner has tacit permission to stop the conference at any time, drawing the audience's in-the-moment attention to particularly relevant transactions occurring before them.

- **Duet**

  This is the epitome of exemplary copresenting. This fifth form carefully blends several ingredients to produce maximum effect with minimum display of effort. Both presenters are onstage at the same time. They balance the stage: one stands on the right, the other on the left. When one moves to the left to make a point, the other drifts unobtrusively to the right. They choreograph their movements. The speaker avoids blocking the recorder's visuals. Just as in tennis doubles, they play the net: one forward, the other back, one embedded in the audience space, the other on stage. The following are some ways you can recognize copresenters operating as a duet:

  1. Presenters employ brief content chunks. One talks briefly, for thirty seconds to two minutes; then the other talks briefly.
  2. They may finish sentences for each other. First presenter: "And you should know that ..." Second presenter: "the first consideration is trust."
  3. They use physical proximity as a tool. Copresenter duets do best when they stand three to seven feet apart.

4. They subtly cue each other with looks, proximity, hand gestures, voice tempo, and intonation.
5. They stay focused all the time, each attentive to the other and the audience. A participant once told Suzanne and me that when one of us was speaking, the other looked as if the most interesting presenter in the world were speaking. We model rapt attention to each other's words. It's as if we were hearing the words for the first time.
6. They use a synchronistic style—the mutual telling of a story, exchanging speaker roles every other line or so, sometimes speaking together at the same time.
7. Copresenters who are attentive to their own development will change who delivers what content as well as their style of content delivery, so each time is really the first time the words are spoken.

Getting Started

All five copresenting methods can produce exciting results, but only if both people work compatibly and understand the basic ground rules that keep copresentations orderly. That's the first order of business.

Several interpersonal factors contribute to a team's success as copresenters. The most important is agreement on key issues: beliefs concerning adults as learners, training philosophy, orientation to the topic, strategies for coplanning, and approaches to resolving problems together. Consider the problems that face a team when one partner tries to contribute to sessions by controlling his or her feelings while the other person tries to promote harmony by using and expressing feelings. They're headed for trouble unless they can discuss their communication approaches and arrive at a commonly understood strategy together. Such differences in assumptions and style can cause havoc that overrides even the best intentions.

The ability to maintain personal composure plays a tremendous role in copresenting success. No matter how compatible the team, eventually something will threaten, annoy, or embarrass one or both members. We once heard a copresenter come close to revealing a highly personal and embarrassing bit of information about the partner. It took all the composure the partner could muster to stay unthreatened and consciously attuned to the content they were presenting.

On another occasion, we watched a copresenter unexpectedly launch into a diatribe on a favorite topic. This wasn't part of the planned agenda, and if continued, it would have prevented the partner from delivering a previously agreed-upon important portion of content. The partner later reported briefly of feeling unequal, useless, and angry at this insensitivity. It took a lot of composure to get through the balance of this training day. This ability to take charge of one's own emotions relates to the next critical criterion in a good partnership, the matter of discipline.

Discipline is the ability to stick to the agreed-upon design. It's the willingness to monitor oneself and refrain from telling that favorite story if it adds little to the program. Discipline means foregoing the cute line when it does not serve the purpose. It's being able to see that time is short or that the point has been made, and eliminating portions of well-rehearsed content or activities as necessary.

Cutting things short, even when absolutely necessary, can be very difficult. We've observed that presenters who are exceptionally strong at storing workshop content in auditory loops sometimes have a hard time abbreviating content when time is short. This may be because their content is stored in sequence and must be retrieved in a certain order. Some find it hard to cut material when content is new. Sometimes, presenting the content intact becomes more important to the presenter than the effect of the content on the audience. Nonetheless, copresenters must be ready to adjust planned content and activities to meet the unique requirements of each setting, and that takes discipline.

Trust in one another is the final ingredient to a successful copresenting partnership. By this we mean trust in the other person's judgment, trust that he or she intends no harm, and trust that he or she can respond to the unexpected. It also means trust that each will submerge one's own ego and help the other look good.

Copresenter trust is more important than it may appear on the surface. It supports collegiality and becomes a metaphor for the honor and respect the copresenters have for the participants. Audiences probably respond as much to that trust, mutual respect, and collegiality as they do to the content being presented.

In most cases, copresenter trust develops over time and is subject to occasional interruptions. People with a natural affinity for one another probably develop that trust fairly rapidly. Ultimately, though, copresenters develop trust in one another just as they do in other relationships: from experiences together in which consistency, confidentiality, crisis survival, risk taking, understanding, and honest communication occur.

Taking the Platform

Now the team is established. Both presenters agree on philosophy, strategies, and approaches. They know they must maintain personal composure and discipline themselves. They also trust one another. Now they're ready to copresent.

This leap into the training room is a big one, though, and it requires some forethought. Making several agreements ahead of time is recommended.

- **Give Permission**

  Agree that each presenter has permission to do whatever is necessary to meet session goals and maintain audience rapport and resourcefulness. Rapport exists when the audience remains responsive to you. Audiences are resourceful when they seem energetic, capable, and receptive to the material you present. Both rapport and resourcefulness are essential.

  We suggest giving each partner ongoing permission to monitor and intervene even if the interventions are unpredictable. For example, each must know it's okay to tell a joke if the other gets inappropriately serious.

- **Develop Signals**

  Develop signals to help each other out. For "your turn," copresenters use intonation shifts, incomplete sentences, and palms turned up. They use physical proximity or eye contact for "I want to add something." A finger on the wristwatch signals, "We are running out of time."

  Each team should develop and agree to signals that suit its own needs and should agree on how to use them. For example, once one partner signals that time is running out, he or she should leave the other presenter alone. Remember, partners need to trust one another to make the appropriate adjustments.

- **Change Arrangements**

  Agree to change prior agreements if necessary. Just because something worked in Atlanta doesn't mean it will work well in Chicago.

- **There Is No One Correct Way**

  Agree that there is no one correct way to present a concept or teach a skill. When we plan an activity, either before the workshop begins or in a huddle during the presentation, one of us may say, "I think we need to do this." The other may respond, "Yes, and you know, here's another way we could do it." And so it goes. The best copresenters intuitively continue this form of brainstorming, going for at least three ideas. Once three are achieved, ideas become generative, and four, five, six, and seven will then flow easily. From that rich collection, the team can easily and mutually select the course most likely to help them reach the desired outcome.

- **Forge Mutual Understandings**

  Agree on some explicit understandings to support the copresenting relationship. Suzanne and I have found several that serve us well. At all times, we agree, our overriding goal is to produce optimal learning. We each have a responsibility to maintain composure and help the other partner look good. We will do whatever it takes to achieve our desired outcomes, whether that means interrupting each other, running dittos, fixing the furniture, planning during breaks, prospecting with trainees before the session begins, or working with audience members at lunch time to help resolve problems.

Tested Tips

With these agreements in place, most copresenting teams will be in good shape. A few additional tips will pave the way for real success.

Planning forms the basis of the presentation. Before they take the stage, excellent copresenters:

1. work together to determine presentation goals, time allocations, major information areas, and the processes that will promote the goals;
2. separately take responsibility for fleshing out details for the different information areas;
3. develop a training outline with space for initials down the side to designate alternating responsibility for each segment;
4. identify all logistical considerations—charts to be made, materials to be developed, printing to be done—and assign responsibility.

Copresenters need to exchange information and ideas that will help the session. We share strategies that have worked in the past, materials we have developed, and knowledge that we think will enrich the other partner's presentation. In addition, we share vignettes, stories, and metaphors that might help illustrate a training point.

Before the presentation, copresenters should compare their wardrobes to make sure clothing is compatible. Both members should arrive at the training site early to establish rapport and make sure the room can support the session goals.

Afterward, analyze what worked, what didn't, and why. Good copresenters apply this information when planning for future sessions. They also assess their copresenting teamwork and commit to refinements.

Finally, they celebrate and pat themselves on the back. Not every session will go perfectly, but copresenting can be an exciting, effective, and rewarding way to train. It conveys the instructional content, but it goes deeper too. The very presence of two people instead of one can be a metaphor for the message. Copresenting communicates collegiality, collaboration, and peer learning. Copresenters communicate about being human, allow little mistakes to show, and laugh with the audience.

When Suzanne and I copresent, we try to signal that we are all learners. That's an important metaphor, no matter what the topic.

End Notes

Crum, T. (1987). *The Magic of Conflict: Turning a Life of Work into a Work of Art*. New York: Simon and Schuster.

Garmston, R. & Bailey, S. (1988). Paddling together: A copresenting primer. *Training and Development Journal,* 42(1): 52–57.

Garmston, R. and Wellman, B. (1992). *How to Make Presentations That Teach and Transform*. Alexandria, VA: Association for Supervision and Curriculum Development.

Lipshitz, R., Friedman, V., & Omer, H. (1989). Overcoming resistance to training: A nonconfrontive approach. *Training and Development Journal* 43 (12): 46–50.

O'Hanlon, W.H. (1987). *Taproots: Underlying Principles of Milton Erickson's Therapy and Hypnosis*. New York: W. W. Norton & Company.

Smith, R. (1984). *Making Successful Presentations: A Self-Teaching Guide*. New York: John Wiley & Sons, Inc.

Turk, C. (1985). *Effective Speaking: Communicating in Speech.* New York: E.& F.N. Spon.

L
H
TAXI
21

POSTSCRIPT

The schools in which you and I work are fast-moving and complex. Our world is even more so. While my experience in Africa was in sharp contrast to the busy distractions of North American life, the vision and ideals I had time to reflect on during safari remain steadfast—to create environments in which each inhabitant of the school is a respected and able learner, and to create work environments of adaptivity, generativity, and heart. To meet the demands of schooling in the twenty-first century, we require work cultures in which entire faculties learn from their experiences and modify practices and policies based upon reflection, values, and vision. Many authors are envisioning and locating examples of such organizations. Some examples are Thomas Sergiovanni in *Leadership for the Schoolhouse* (1996), Peter Senge in *The Fifth Discipline* (1990), Carl Glickman in *Renewing American Schools* (1993), Peter Block in *Stewardship* (1993), Jack Hawley in *Reawakening the Spirit of Work* (1993), and Marvin Weisbord in *Productive Workplaces* (1991).

Art Costa and I, in *Cognitive Coaching* (1994), have described schools in which the values and mediational skills for such self-directed learning occur at all levels within the organization. Bruce Wellman and I are working with schools throughout North America on the practical nuts and bolts of how to achieve Renaissance status. We call such schools *adaptive schools* (Garmston and Wellman, 1995, 1996). By whatever name, these are schools that value learning, schools in which leaders are learners, and schools in which presentations for learning are conducted by everyone. Everyone is a presenter, facilitator, consultant, and coach.

Our work toward these ends is not, however, straightforward and linear. Although we desire transformation, it cannot be achieved as directly or dramatically as sending our teachers on safari in the Serengeti. The goals of staff development must truly embody the dispositions, capacities, and ideals described in Chapter 1 for all adult learners. This work involves examining and challenging our assumptions and mental models about schools as places of learning, the nature of learning, and the ways in which it is supported, stimulated and nurtured.

One important step on this learning journey is to stop pretending that we are apart from the universe and exist as engineers, mechanics, mothers, or fathers who can see what is wrong and fix it. Not everything is fixable; not everything is motherable. In fact, some situations react violently and unpredictably to being mothered, fathered, or fixed.

As I whimsically wrote one winter after trying to get to a National Staff Development Conference in an unusually severe storm:

> We are instead in the hurricane, wind, and snow whipping across highway 94, heading east and south from Minneapolis to Chicago. Forty-one below zero wind chill factor, all flights canceled, taxi the only way across the 400 miles separating the two cities. Semis and four-wheel drives, Hondas and Fords make their way in the night. Like steaming locust shells, the bodies of their interiors still warm from their reckless drive, some lay abandoned on the wintry gums of the icy highway.
>
> But yet we persevere, determined to meet our responsibilities, present at the annual NSDC conference to the 125 people who have scheduled themselves for this three day seminar. And so we push. Courageous and linear, determined and single minded. Complete this journey. Do it on schedule, arriving in the dead of night before the advertised workshop. And so we do. And while we travel, relentlessly pushing on, seven miles at one point in thirty-two minutes, drawing deeply from our emotional and physical reserves—and fiscal resources as well, for a midwinter 400-mile cab ride does not come inexpensively—while we push on, the 125 people for whom this Herculean effort is being performed are also on their way to Chicago.
>
> Actually, eighteen of them live in the Chicago area and are already sleeping peacefully in their own beds as we make this journey. Another sixty registrants are trying to reach Chicago from their homes in Wisconsin, Minnesota, Michigan, and other midwestern states. Unfortunately, they are caught in the same storm, and cannot leave home—flights are canceled. From the eastern seaboard, another contingent. From the west, another. A few begin their journey from the far north, Canada and Alaska.

But they all must pass through O'Hare. Clogged artery of the air transportation system, tonight it swirls in snow flurries, sharp winds creating periodic white out across empty runways. Planes can take off, but none can land.

And so we arrive, our goal a product of linear thought and action: get there at any cost. Yet on arrival, we find that the same conditions that challenged us to the limit of our energy have also modified the future toward which we were moving. Fewer than twenty people sit forlornly in a seminar room. The conference, this session and others, is crippled. Materials have not arrived. Neither has the conference.

We are, as the story suggests, in the hurricane. What do we make of it? Two postures seem reasonable to consider if we could begin at this beginning again. First, is there anything we can fix, modify, correct, or improve in the Midwest storm descending on travelers that Friday night? Is there any history we can rewrite about how schools got the way they are? Can we get a different set of students to teach or administrators with whom to work? If the answer is no, we cannot change the past, then we must consider a set of lenses and tools designed to accommodate a difficult situation and achieve as much stability as possible.

Should we accept the challenge to take on the existing situation? We ask ourselves if we are working with a "tame problem" that can be resolved with tested algorithms. Or, is it a "wicked problem," nonlinear in nature, unpredictable in response to interventions we might apply? Based on our analysis here, we select from a repertoire of different tools, one set for tame problems, one for wicked.

The twentieth century Western mind has the most experience with tame problems and the greatest collection of models, tools, and navigational aides with which to address them. These models and tools have taken us to the moon, discovered the Salk vaccine, invented universal schooling, conducted the Gulf War, launched cyberspace, and created technological revolutions.

Yet our collected wisdom stands powerless against homelessness, poverty, school failure, the assaults of radical groups upon the establishment, scheduling secondary students for different times for different subjects, implementing comprehensive and common-sense assessment systems for students, and balancing the budget. These are wicked problems for which no linear problem-solving paradigms exist.

Our first glimpse of wisdom may be to realize that to create adaptive schools requires addressing a different class of problems that requires different approaches. Indeed, they are not problems at all, in the conventional use of the term, where the word *problem* presumes a solution. These, instead, might more properly be termed conditions, undesirable conditions for which alternative conditions are being sought.

This way of thinking takes us to several models for addressing these challenges. One is to engage ourselves and our communities in a dialogue (to inquire, to understand) on what we are about. Another step is to recognize that we desire something different than what we have. So we envision a desired state: first, in global terms—for example, schools as learning organizations—then, to the degree that we can, in behavioral terms.

During the late 1980s and well into the 1990s, movement occurred in schools and business organizations in which learning from experience by all the inhabitants of a work culture would effect continuous change in policy, practice, and effectiveness. Peter Senge (1990) described such phenomena as "learning organizations"—organizations that are continually expanding their capacity to create their future.

Laura Lipton and I (1997) have described such schools as developmental, evolving organizations that are engaged in shared reflection about larger (wider, deeper, and more abstract) purposes. These schools focus on developing the intellectual capacity that is required for sound individual and collective decision making about instruction.

Many are working to support the achievement of the vision of schools that are adaptive and capable of changing their form but that clarify and maintain their identity in serving students. Such schools continually invest in production capacity, increasing the organization's ability to learn—and change—from critical reflection about its experiences (Garmston and Wellman, 1995, 1996).

For over a decade Art Costa and I (Costa and Garmston, 1994) have worked to support schools in constructing a foundation of reflective and mediational skills, exercised by all the players, that we believe are necessary to achieve such schools. The schools of which we dream, and in some communities are realizing, represent a "rebirth and awakening, a reenergizing of values, a reconnecting with natural forces found in the universe, a recognition of the innate capacities for human development, both individually and in groups ... at once a celebration of the limitless potential and creativity of the human spirit and a means of continuous improvement towards ideals" (Costa and Garmston, 1994). We believe that educational organizations that embody these characteristics are vitally important to our continued evolution as a nation. In this endeavor we are in good company. I take heart that there are many others, minds far better and more influential than mine, who also seem to support this general direction.

Among these are Carl Glickman, Thomas Sergiovanni, John Goodlad, Michael Fullan, Linda Lambert, William Glasser, Seymour Sarason, Sarah Lawrence Lightfoot, Milbrey McLaughlin, Judith Warren Little, and Ronald Barth.

And so, let us return to the beginning. Chapter 1 described this book's purpose as an exploration of how presentations and presenters can support us in transforming ourselves, our schools, and our future possibilities. I reported that who we think we are (our identity) drives all our beliefs, values, capabilities, and behaviors. Now it is time to reveal that what has even greater influence, and what informs identity, lives on a spiritual plane—our sense of connection with and personal mission in this world. I believe that, guided by our best instincts, we become united as inquirers and collaborators, making schools, and the world, better for children—and for all of us.

End Notes

Block, P. (1993). *Stewardship: Choosing Service over Self-Interest*. San Francisco: Berrett-Kaehler Publishers.

Costa, A. & Garmston, R. (1994). *Cognitive coaching: A Foundation for Renaissance Schools*. Norwood, MA: Christopher-Gordon Publishers, Inc.

Garmston, R. & Lipton, L. (1997). The psychology of supervision: From behaviorism to constructivism. In Gerald Firth and Edward Pajak. (eds.) *The Handbook of Research on School Supervision*. New York: Macmillan Library Reference, A Division of Simon and Schuster, Inc.

Garmston, R. & Wellman, B. (1995). Adaptive schools in a quantum universe. *Educational Leadership* 52(7): 6–12.

Garmston, R. & Wellman, B. (1996). *Adaptive School: Developing and Facilitating Collaborative Groups*. Mansfield, OH: Bookmasters, Inc.

Glickman, C. (1993). *Renewing American Schools: A Guide for School-based Action*. San Francisco: Jossey-Bass.

Hawley, J. (1993). *Reawakening the Spirit of Work: The Power of Dharmic Management*. San Francisco: Berrett-Kaehler Publishers.

Senge, P. (1990). *The Fifth Discipline: The Art and Practice of the Learning Organization*. New York: Doubleday.

Sergiovanni, T. (1996). *Leadership for the Schoolhouse: How Is It Different? Why Is It Important?*. San Francisco: Jossey-Bass.

Weisbord, M. (1991). *Productive Workplaces: Organizing and Managing for Dignity, Meaning and Community*. San Francisco: Jossey-Bass.

VIEW

REFERENCES

Allen, S. & Wollman, J. (1987). *How to Be Funny: Discovering the Comic You*. New York: McGraw-Hill.

Armstrong, D. (1992) *Management by Storying Around: A New Method of Leadership*. New York: Doubleday.

Austin, N. & Peters, T. (1985). *A Passion for Excellence*. New York: Random House.

Bailey, S. (1993). *Stories and metaphors for change agents*. Unpublished paper presented at the Association for Supervision and Curriculum Development Institute, Boston.

Berman, P. & McLaughlin, M. (1980). Factors affecting the process of change. In M. Milstein (ed.), *Schools, Conflicts and Change*. New York: Teachers College Press.

Berry, S. E. & Garmston, R. J. (1987). Become a state-of-the-art presenter. *Training and Development Journal* 41(1): 19–23.

Block, P. (1993). *Stewardship: Choosing Service over Self-Interest*. San Francisco: Berrett-Kaehler Publishers.

Brickey, M. (1991). Making changes by changing identity. *Anchor Point* 5(11): 1–4.

Bridges, W. (1980). *Transitions: Making Sense of Life's Changes*. New York: Addison-Wesley.

Bridges, W. (1991). *Managing Transitions: Making the Most of Change*. New York: Addison-Wesley.

Buck, C. (1986). Humorless election year is nothing to laugh at. *The Sacramento Bee,* May 26. Sacramento, CA.

Buckley, H. (1961). *The Little Boy*. Bradenton, FL: Helen Buckley.

Campbell, J. (1987). *Primitive Mythology: The Masks of God*. New York: Penguin.

Campbell, J. (1988). *Historical Atlas of World Mythology*. New York: Harper & Row.

Canfield, J. & Hansen, M.V. (1993). *Chicken Soup for the Soul: 101 Stories to Open the Heart and Rekindle the Spirit*. Deerfield Beach, FL: Health Communications, Inc.

Cathcart, J. (1995). Customize your style and content to fit your audience. In Members of Speakers' Roundtable (eds.), *Speaking Secrets of the Masters: The Speakers' Roundtable.* Harrisburg, PA: Executive Books.

Chopra, D. (1990). *Quantum Healing: Exploring the Frontiers of Mind/Body Medicine.* New York: Bantam Books.

Costa, A. (1991). The school as a home for the mind. In A. Costa (ed.), *Developing Minds: A Resource Book for Teaching Thinking.* Alexandria, VA: Association for Supervision and Curriculum Development.

Costa, A. (1991). The search for intelligent life. In A. Costa (ed.), *Developing Minds: A Resource Book for Teaching Thinking,* Vol. 1. Alexandria, VA: Association for Supervision and Curriculum Development.

Costa, A. (1991). Some thoughts on transfer. Unpublished paper. Berkeley, CA: Institute for Intelligent Behavior.

Costa, A. & Garmston, R. (1994). *Cognitive Coaching: A Foundation for Renaissance Schools.* Norwood, MA: Christopher-Gordon Publishers, Inc.

Costa, A. & Garmston, R. (In press). Maturing outcomes. *Educational Leadership.*

Covey, S. (1989). *The Seven Habits of Highly Effective People.* New York: Simon & Schuster.

Crum, T. (1987). *The Magic of Conflict: Turning a Life of Work into a Work of Art.* New York: Simon and Schuster.

Decialdini, R. (1984). *The New Psychology of Modern Persuasion.* New York: Simon & Schuster.

Deighton, L. (1962). *The Ipcress File.* New York: Ballantine Books.

Dilts, R. (1989). *Pathways to Leadership Seminar Booklet.* Santa Cruz, CA: Dynamic Learning Center.

Dilts, R.B. (1994). *Effective Presentation Skills.* Capitola, CA: Meta Publications.

Doyle, M. & Strauss, D. (1993). *How to Make Meetings Work: The New Interaction Method.* New York: Berkeley Publishing Group.

Eitington, J. (1984). *The Winning Trainer.* Houston, TX: Gulf Publishing Co.

Elgin, S.H. (1990). *Staying Well with the Gentle Art of Verbal Self-Defense.* Englewood Cliffs, NJ: Prentice Hall.

Elmore, R.F. (1995). Structural reform and educational practice. *Educational Researcher* 24(9): 23–26.

Elmore, R.F. & Fuhrman, S.H. (eds.). (1994). *The Governance of Curriculum: The 1994 ASCD Yearbook.* Alexandria, VA: Association for Supervision and Curriculum Development.

Ewing, I. (1994). *The Best Presentation Skills.* Singapore: Ewing Communications Pte Ltd.

Faulkner, C. (1991). *Metaphors of Identity: Operating Metaphors and Iconic Change* (cassette recording). Cleveland: Genesis II.

Fripp, P. (1995). *You've Got to Be Lively: Speaking Secrets of the Masters* Harrisburg, PA: Executive Books.

Fullan, M. (1993). *Change Forces: Probing the Depths of Educational Reform.* Bristol, PA: Falmer Press.

Garmston, R. (1991). Staff developers as social architects. *Educational Leadership* 49(3): 64–65.

Garmston, R. & Bailey, S. (1988). Paddling together: A copresenting primer. *Training and Development Journal* 42(1): 52–57.

Garmston, R. & Lipton, L. (1997). The psychology of supervision: From behaviorism to constructivism. In Firth and Pajak (ed.) *The Handbook of Research on School Supervision.* New York: MacMillan.

Garmston, R. & Wellman, B. (1992). *How to Make Presentations That Teach and Transform.* Alexandria, VA: Association for Supervision and Curriculum Development.

Garmston, R. & Wellman, B. (1995). Adaptive schools in a quantum universe. *Educational Leadership* 52(7): 6–12.

Garmston, R. & Wellman, B. (1996). *Adaptive School: Developing and Facilitating Collaborative Groups.* El Dorado Falls, CA: Four Hats Press.

Gibb, J.R. (1978). *Trust: A New View of Personal and Organizational Development.* Los Angeles: Guild of Tutors Press.

Glickman, C. (1993). *Renewing American Schools: A Guide for School-Based Action.* San Francisco: Jossey-Bass.

Gordon, D. (1978). *Therapeutic Metaphors.* Cupertino, CA: Meta Publications.

Grinder, M. (1993). *Envoy: Your Personal Guide to Classroom Management.* Battle Ground, WA: Michael Grinder & Associates.

Hawley, J. (1993). *Reawakening the Spirit of Work: The Power of Dharmic Management.* San Francisco: Berrett-Kaehler Publishers.

Jaccaci, A.T. (1989). The social architecture of a learning culture. *Training and Development Journal* 43(11): 50–53.

Johnson, D., & Johnson, R. (1994). Constructive conflict in the schools. *Journal of Social Issues* 50(1): 117–137.

Jones, R. (1982). *Physics As Metaphor.* New York: Meridian.

Joyce, B. & Showers, B. (1988). *Student Achievement through Staff Development.* New York: Longman.

Kegan, R. (1982). *The Evolving Self: Problem and Process in Human Development.* Cambridge, MA: Harvard University Press.

Kofman, F. & Senge, P. (1993). Communities of commitment: The heart of learning organizations. *Organizational Dynamics* (Autumn): 5–23.

Kouzes, J.M. & Posner, B.Z. (1993). *Credibility: How Leaders Gain and Lose It, Why People Demand It.* San Francisco: Jossey-Bass.

Lamb, S. (1980). *Hemispheric specialization and storytelling: Implications and applications for longstanding problems.* Unpublished master's thesis, University of California, Los Angeles.

Lambert, L. (1995). *The Constructivist Leader.* New York: Teachers College Press.

Lipshitz, R., Friedman, V., & Omer, H. (1989). Overcoming resistance to training: A nonconfrontive approach. *Training and Development Journal* 43 (12): 46–50.

Lipton, L. (1996). Making Learning Meaningful: Strategic Teaching for Connectedness. Unpublished manuscript.

McPhee, D. (1992). Music: Easy and fast way to accelerate learning. *AL&T Network Newsletter* 1(1): 1–2.

Mills, J. & Crowley, R. (1986). *Therapeutic Metaphors for Children and the Child Within.* New York: Bruner/Mazel.

Nickerson, S. (1995). Breaking the language barrier. *Training and Development Journal* 49(2): 45–48.

Noonan, P. (1990). *What I Saw at the Revolution: A Political Life in the Reagan Era.* New York: Random House.

O'Connor, J. & Seymour, J. (1990). *Introducing Neuro-linguistic Programming: The New Psychology of Personal Excellence.* London: Mandala.

O'Hanlon, W.H. (1987). *Taproots: Underlying Principles of Milton Erickson's Therapy and Hypnosis.* New York: W. W. Norton & Company.

Ornstein, R. (1991). *The Evolution of Consciousness.* New York: Prentice Hall.

Pedersen, D. (1990). Unpublished manuscript. Sacramento, CA: California State University.

Perkins, D. & Salomon, G. (1991). Teaching for transfer. In A. Costa (ed.), *Developing Minds: A Resource Book for Teaching Thinking.* Alexandria, VA: Association for Supervision and Curriculum Development.

Peters, T.J. & Waterman, R.H., Jr. (1982). *In Search of Excellence: Lessons from America's Best-Run Companies.* New York: Harper & Row.

Pyramid Film & Video (producer). (1992). *Project Star: A Private Universe.* Santa Monica, CA: Pyramid Film & Video.

Rosenholtz, S.S. (1989). *Teachers' Workplace: The Social Organization of Schools.* New York: Longman.

Rowe, M.B. (1986). Wait time: Slowing down may be a way of speeding up! *Journal of Teacher Education* 23: 43–49.

Saphier, J. & Gower, R. (1987). *The Skillful Teacher: Building Your Teaching Skills.* Carlisle, MA: Research for Better Teaching, Inc.

Senge, P. (1990). *The Fifth Discipline: The Art and Practice of the Learning Organization.* New York: Doubleday.

Sergiovanni, T. (1996). *Leadership for the Schoolhouse: How is it Different? Why is it Important?* San Francisco: Jossey-Bass.

Shipley, J.T. (1959). *Dictionary of Word Origins.* Ames, IA: Littlefield, Adams & Co.

Sinetar, M. (1991). *Developing a 21st Century Mind.* New York: Villard Books.

Smith, R. (1984). *Making Successful Presentations: A Self-Teaching Guide.* New York: John Wiley & Sons, Inc.

Sparks, D. (1990). Cognitive coaching: An interview with Robert Garmston. *Journal of Staff Development,* 11(2): 12–15.

Sprinthall, N. & Theis-Sprinthall, L. (1983). The teacher as an adult learner: A cognitive development view. In G. Griffin (ed.), *Staff Development: Eighty-second Yearbook of the National Society for the Study of Education.* Chicago: University of Chicago Press.

Stone, I. (1956). *Men to Match My Mountains.* New York: Doubleday.

True, H. (1995). The power of humor. *Speaking Secrets of the Masters.* Harrisburg, PA: Executive Books.

Turk, C. (1985). *Effective speaking: Communicating in Speech.* New York: E. & F.N. Spon.

Von Oech, R. (1983). *A Whack on the Side of the Head.* New York: Warner Books.

Weisbord, M. (1991). *Productive Workplaces: Organizing and Managing for Dignity, Meaning and Community.* San Francisco: Jossey-Bass.

Wellman, B. & Lipton, L. (1991). Making meaning: Linking primary science and literature. Presented at the Association for Supervision and Curriculum Development National Conference, San Francisco.

Whitmore, J. (1994). *Coaching for Performance: A Practical Guide for Growing Your Own Skills.* London: Nicholas Brealey Publishing, Ltd.

Weiner, A. (1989). *Speak with impact seminar*. Sherman Oaks, CA: Communication Development Associates, Inc.

Wohlmuth, E. (1983). *The Overnight Guide to Public Speaking*. Philadelphia: Running Press.

ABOUT THE AUTHOR

Dr. Robert J. Garmston, Professor Emeritus of Educational Administration at California State University, Sacramento, is Executive Director of Facilitation Associates, and Educational consulting firm specializing in leadership, learning, and personal and organizational development. He is co-developer of Cognitive Coaching and Co-Director of the Institute for Intelligent Behavior with Dr. Arthur Costa. Dr. Garmston is the author of numerous publications on leadership, supervision, and staff development. He has made presentations and conducted workshops for educators, managers and professional trainers throughout the United States and in Canada, Europe, Asia, Africa, and Middle East. He received his Ed. in Educational Administration from the University of Southern California. He lives near Sacramento, California with his wife Sue, and close to his children Kimberly, Judy, Kevin, Michael and Wendy.

ABOUT THE ILLUSTRATOR

Michael Buckley has worked in New England as an illustrator, graphic designer and fine artist since 1980. His graphic work has appeared in numerous publications, on labels and logos, as well as posters and tee shirts, His drawings and paintings are exhibited and collected locally, nationally and internationally. He currently resides outside New York City, where he teaches, paints, draws, and occasionally collaborates on special projects such as this one.

INDEX